Scotland: A Very Short Introduction

Titles in the series include the following:

Rab Houston

SCOTLAND

A Very Short Introduction

OXFORD
UNIVERSITY PRESS

Great Clarendon Street, Oxford OX2 6DP

Oxford University Press is a department of the University of Oxford.
It furthers the University's objective of excellence in research, scholarship,
and education by publishing worldwide in

Oxford New York

Auckland Cape Town Dar es Salaam Hong Kong Karachi
Kuala Lumpur Madrid Melbourne Mexico City Nairobi
New Delhi Shanghai Taipei Toronto

With offices in

Argentina Austria Brazil Chile Czech Republic France Greece
Guatemala Hungary Italy Japan Poland Portugal Singapore
South Korea Switzerland Thailand Turkey Ukraine Vietnam

Oxford is a registered trade mark of Oxford University Press
in the UK and in certain other countries

Published in the United States
by Oxford University Press Inc., New York

British Library Cataloguing in Publication Data

Data available

Library of Congress Cataloging in Publication Data

Data available

ISBN 978-0-19-923079-2

Typeset by SPI Publisher Services, Pondicherry, India
Printed and bound by CPI Group (UK) Ltd, Croydon, CR0 4YY

To the memory of my mother,
Janet Paterson Houston (née Brown),
1920–2007.

Contents

List of illustrations

The publisher and the author apologize for any errors or omissions in the above list. If contacted they will be pleased to rectify these at the earliest opportunity.

Early kingdoms and peoples

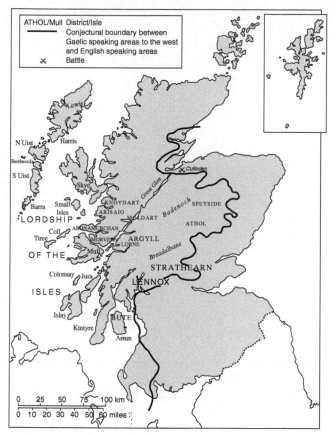

ATHOL/Mull District/Isle
⎯⎯⎯ Conjectural boundary between
Gaelic speaking areas to the west
and English speaking areas
✕ Battle

Lewis
N Uist
Harris
Benbecula
S Uist
Skye
Barra   Small
         Isles
Tiree   Coll
LORDSHIP
         KNOYDART
         ARISAIG
         ARDNAMURCHAN   MOIDART   Badenoch   SPEYSIDE
         MORVERN   LORNE   ATHOL
OF THE   Mull   ARGYLL
                  Breadalbane
Colonsay   Jura   STRATHEARN
ISLES   LENNOX
Islay
         BUTE
Kintyre
         Arran

Great Glen
✕ Culloden

0   25   50   75   100 km
0 10 20 30 40 50 60 miles

The historic Highlands and Western Isles

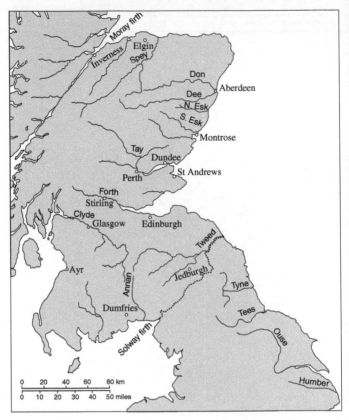

The main towns and rivers of Scotland and The rivers of north-east England

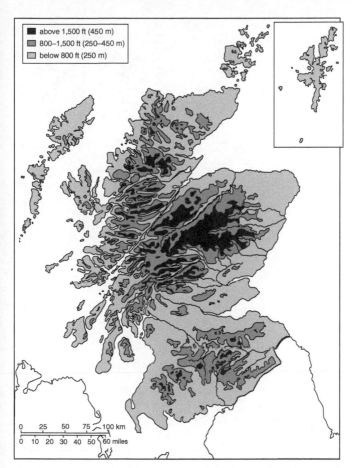

Physical map of Scotland

The pre-1975 administrative regions of Scotland

Introduction

Britons and non-Britons alike often find it hard to grasp what Scotland is about. Are the Scots really just a sort of English? The answer is an emphatic 'No'. Is Scotland a distinctive entity within Britain? 'Yes'. Are the Scots British? 'Sometimes'. Scotland and England share a language, a monarch (since 1603), and a parliament (since 1707), and they went through shared experiences of empire and industrial revolution. Yet many other aspects of their history have made them very different. George Orwell once wrote in 'England, your England': 'National characteristics are not easy to pin down, and when pinned down they often turn out to be trivialities or seem to have no connexion with one another.'

The connections again lie in history. The social, political, and cultural characteristics of modern Scots come out of centuries of separate and parallel development within a British and European context. Theirs is a story of continuities and change, of consistency and contradiction, of good and bad, but what distinguishes Scotland is its experience of government, religion, law, education, social relationships, population mobility, and culture. Only by explaining and evaluating this history can we understand Scotland's present.

Four themes run through this study. First, while Scotland is not obviously 'multi-cultural' by modern standards, it has historically been marked by pronounced geographic, linguistic, religious, and social differences remarkable in so small a country. Second, it developed and has a strong 'civil society' or 'voluntary sector' that has at times reinforced those differences and at others created homogeneity of vision, notably in ideas about education and common humanity. Third, whatever the local and regional differences, Scotland developed a sense of national identity during the Middle Ages that has never dimmed, even within the context of Union with England and even when Scots exalted in being 'British'.

The final theme concerns what it means to be both Scottish and British. The misunderstandings (and sometimes antagonisms) between modern Scots and English come out of a tension between their shared experience and the desire to remain different. Scots (and English) are only 'British' in specific contexts and appeals to this level of identity include sectional characteristics rather than overriding them. When Scots (or Welsh or northern Irish) talk of themselves as 'British', they draw on a long history of being different as well as a limited experience of being the same – though they are more likely to use the word inclusively than are the English. Nationalist histories of post-1922 Ireland and of post-revolutionary America are convincing because they broke free of the (English) imposition of a British culture and government. Scots never did and arguably most never wanted to, partly because they had a more positive role in making that culture.

England is not the only country with which Scotland had interactions and it has not always been the most important one. Nevertheless, Scottish and English (and Irish) history have been intertwined for centuries and Scots have participated in a British project, embracing Union with varying degrees of enthusiasm and reserve. Scottish history needs to be understood with English history, not to see what was overlaid, repressed, and distorted by an alien English imposition, but to understand what was separate and what was shared. British history is a part of Scottish history regardless of whether Scotland remains a part of the United Kingdom in the future.

Chapter 1
Politics and government

Making Britain

To see Britain as Scotland, England, and Wales is to accept a medieval creation, for until then there was nothing inevitable about the emergence of a separate and independent Scottish realm. For centuries there was a chance that the fragmented political units of Dark Age Scotland might either have remained disunited or have been brought together under English control.

The Dark Age land that is now Scotland was a shifting patchwork of political alliances and peoples that comprised three main groupings. Dál Riata (focused on Argyllshire in the west) belonged to the 'Scots' (an English word with no Scottish vernacular form, best translated as 'Gaels'), a people also found in Ireland. The Picts occupied the north and east and the Britons the south. Both then and far into the Middle Ages, Scotland resembled Wales and Ireland, a loose-knit ensemble of separate chiefs or lords with limited chances of cohering into anything larger and more potent.

Integration proceeded only slowly. In 843, a Pictish king, Kenneth MacAlpin (Cinaed mac Alpín), united Scotland north of the Forth into what eventually became known c. 900 as 'Alba'. The political focus moved from Argyllshire to Perthshire in the east as the composite kingdom joined Scots or Gaels with Picts, though ultimately Gaelic influences eclipsed Pictish. The next landmark was in 1018 when King Malcolm II defeated the Northumbrians (who had controlled much of south-east Scotland since the 7th century) to bring Lothian under his control. Yet even then parts of the north and west still had independent Scandinavian-run administrations, for Viking raiders had carved out their own territories in Scotland (and Ireland) since c. 800. Comprising two interlocking kingdoms in 1100, Alba encompassed only a third of modern Scotland, with Northumbria, stretching across south-east Scotland and north-east England, and the Norse-dominated kingdom of the Isles to the west composing the rest.

Monarchs began to call themselves 'king of Scots' in the 12th century, and during the 13th century Scotland's borders became firmer and its political focus clearer. Northumbria remained a buffer zone: Berwick-upon-Tweed changed hands 13 times between 1147 and 1482, since when it has remained English. Indeed, English kings accepted a measure of territorial semi-detachment, sometimes not feeling invaded until Scots troops reached the River Tees or even the Humber on their frequent incursions. It only became clear that Northumbria south of the Tweed would remain English when in 1237, in the Treaty of York, King Alexander II gave up two centuries of claims to the northern English counties. This treaty consolidated an Anglo-Scottish peace that lasted from 1217 to 1296 and allowed monarchs to work on assimilating Galloway to the emerging Scottish state, yet it remained semi-detached until the 15th century.

Alexander II's reign marked a major shift in the focus of Scottish kings, who gave up the chance to redraw the political map of Britain and sought henceforth to expand their reach to the north and west rather than the south. Alexander died trying to wrest the Hebrides and the Isle of Man from the Norwegian king, a task eventually achieved by his son Alexander III after the Battle of Largs (Ayrs., 1263). Thus by 1266, by virtue of the Treaty of Perth,

'Britain' (excluding the then separate principality of Wales) comprised two separate centralizing monarchies with more-or-less clearly defined territories. The other was England, which had become unified much earlier than Scotland. By AD 1000 at the latest, it had ceased to be a loose grouping of small kingdoms and became a 'united kingdom' with its centre of gravity in the south-east: the unitary Anglo-Saxon 'state' of 'Engla Lond'.

In hindsight, the unifying forces within Scotland were as clear as was its separation from England. But the development of a united and independent Scottish kingdom was far from inevitable. Instead, there were countervailing influences that might have promoted fuller *British* integration under English lordship. During the 12th and 13th centuries, Scotland and England grew closer in two important ways. For one thing, their dynasties became linked. For another, Norman barons like Bruce, Balliol, and Stewart, later to provide kings of Scotland in their own right, were invited in by King David I and established across Lowland Scotland during the 12th century. This settlement was part of a wider process by which much of Britain and Ireland gradually became Normanized after the Norman Conquest of England in 1066.

Norman influence was most pronounced in Scotland under David I, who carried his long experience of the Norman court and culture into his search to extend royal authority, not only by planting Norman barons, but also by introducing written records, building castles, and creating boroughs or 'burghs' with chartered trading privileges and corporate administrations. Yet these were adopted voluntarily rather than imposed from outside, for there was no Norman Conquest of Scotland. That England was already an integrated state in 1066 had made it easier to take over and to change. Scotland was a different kind of entity. Politically decentralized then and for centuries afterwards, it was Normanized by immigration and assimilation, not force.

1. Castles were distinctive Anglo-Norman introductions, symbols of power and status as well as centres of government in the Middle Ages

Breaking Britain: the Wars of Independence

Unlike medieval England, Wales, and Ireland, Scotland was never a wholly conquered country, but there were times when it was a close-run thing. Scotland had important ties with England and might in time have come fully (perhaps even peacefully) within the orbit of English kings. Paradoxically, political, social, and military changes brought about by Anglo-Norman overlordship ultimately laid the foundations of an independent Scotland. In particular, the wars begun by English King Edward I (1272–1307) and continued by his successors obliged a single aristocracy (often with lands in both Scotland and England) to decide where their loyalty lay, confirming not only Scottishness, but also Englishness. Along the way, the Anglo-Norman lords of the 12th-century Lowlands joined with their Gaelic counterparts in the Highlands (the mountainous part of north and west Scotland) to become a separate Scottish aristocracy. The very forces of integration in the 12th and 13th

8

centuries drove Scotland and England apart in the 14th century and ultimately sealed their futures as independent countries.

Edward I claimed (among others) the lands of Wales and Ireland. He administered Ireland, conquered Wales (though it was only integrated with England by the Tudors), and, as the most powerful king in Britain, he exercised direct and superior lordship over Scotland. He therefore seemed close to creating a single British kingdom. Following the death of King Alexander III's heir, Margaret, in 1290, Edward oversaw hearings of the 'Great Cause' (the succession issue), which put John Balliol (John I) on the Scottish throne in 1292. Edward's British vision looked like being realized. But Scotland sought out the French as a counterweight to England, forging in 1295 a bond (the 'Auld [old] Alliance') that endured until the 16th century. By then, England had long been the 'auld enemy' (Chapter 6).

Tensions escalated. In 1296, small cross-border raids by the Scots caused Edward to mount a full-scale invasion, starting what became known to Scots as the 'Wars of Independence'. He slaughtered his way through Berwick and Dunbar, took Edinburgh and Stirling castles, and then went as far north as Elgin. Early military opposition was led by William Wallace, but he ended up a friendless outlaw, eventually hanged, drawn, and quartered in London in 1305. Edward could then claim a geographically extensive, increasingly uniform, and possibly effective rule over all parts of the British Isles, with ultimate judicial, legislative, fiscal, and administrative control from London.

But his hold on Ireland and Scotland proved uncertain and Edward's British state soon unravelled. From 1306, a complex train of events found Robert Bruce, earl of Carrick, leading opposition to the English and ultimately claiming the crown of Scotland. Bruce won a stunning victory against a much larger English force in the two-day battle at Bannockburn (Stirlings.) in 1314. The Scots used their 'common' or citizen army, based on unpaid but highly committed peasant levies, in tightly packed contingents of pikemen (*schiltrom*) to neutralize enemy cavalry before a surprise attack routed the English. The immediate result was the surrender of the English garrison at Stirling castle, but in retrospect the battle was a momentous turning point. Edwardian pretensions remained, but they were unlikely to be realized.

Against the odds, Bruce used his victory and political skill to forge a Scottish nation. For all his virtues, Bruce was a divisive figure among a divided nobility, a violent, self-seeking man who was able to assume the mantle of patriotism. Some of those who sealed an apparently solid bond of support, the famous Declaration of Arbroath (1320), rebelled against him soon after. The Declaration, regarded as a landmark in the making of the Scottish nation, was an appeal to Pope John XXII for assistance by legitimating coronation of an independent ruler, declaiming that 'as long as a hundred of us are left, we will never submit on any condition to English rule. We fight not for glory, riches nor honours, but for freedom...'. Yet Bruce (as King Robert I) cleverly linked his dynasty to the ideal of an independent nation and, with the support of nobles and commoners alike, created a strong new monarchy as a focal point for subsequent Scottish identity.

On the surface, Bannockburn made little lasting difference, for English interference continued, creating an enduring distrust. But in the long term Bannockburn was the most important battle not just in Scottish or English history, but in *British* history, because it marked the end of any serious chance of a 'super-overlordship' of Britain. Given the half-hearted and incomplete medieval conquest of the rest of the British Isles, it is probably a good thing the Scots won so spectacularly. Ireland and Wales came under English sway thanks to 'private enterprise' invasions by Anglo-Norman magnates from the 12th century. The loose ends were tied up for Wales in the 16th century, but never for Ireland, and the indigenous peoples of both suffered from a sort of apartheid. Since the 10th century, policy towards Scotland necessarily came from the English crown, as no noble was strong enough to take on so diverse and divided (and yet so potent) a country. Bannockburn made plain the limits of even the English crown's ambitions and was a landmark in the formation of an independent Scotland.

Making Scotland: from independence to Unions

For all its apparently timeless appeal, the Declaration of Arbroath was specifically a petition for recognition of an independent crown made to the ultimate Christian authority, the papacy. Framed by churchmen as well as laity, it demonstrated the political importance of the Church in Scotland and across Europe. Its focus on royal or regnal liberty was because Scotland at this date was a purely political entity with little to unite it, except the monarch and the Church, and much to divide it. Scotland grew by dynastic accretion, and loyalty to the monarchy helped create a sense of 'nation'. People spoke of the 'community of the realm', but they meant those living under a king.

Indeed, monarchy was the main focus of identity for medieval Scots, even when it was weak. Most 15th-century English kings were usurpers (five dynastic changes occurred 1399–1485), but the house of Stewart descended continuously from Robert II in 1371 until the death of Queen Anne in 1714. The reason for the resilience is that prior to the 16th century the monarchy was more a focal point than a powerful independent actor. Scottish kings preferred to avoid confrontation with their aristocracy, though David II, James I, and James II coped with strong opposition to demands for money. Nor did they impose much direct taxation on their subjects, thus enjoying relative peace compared with contemporary Europe. The nobility had little interest in furthering the ambitions of rulers like James III, who wanted to cut a dash by warring abroad in the 1470s (he died fighting a rebellion in 1488). James IV and V were more successful in extracting money without opposition, though routine royal taxation was not established until James VI's reign.

The ideal of monarchy meant that prolonged minorities did not damage the realm. Mary, Queen of Scots, was a week old when her father James V died. Raised in France from 1548, she married the heir to the French throne in 1558 and did not come to Scotland until after he died; her successor James VI was also an infant when she was deposed in 1567. It was not during a minority, but under adult Mary that the Scottish monarchy reached its lowest ebb. By the time she arrived in Scotland in 1561, a radical 'Reformation' of religion (replacing Catholicism with Protestantism) had been orchestrated by a group of dissident nobles, and she spent her time as queen on damage limitation.

Scotland's aristocrats did not want too strong a monarch, but an ineffective one was just as useless. Mary did reasonably well fending off the strident warnings of Protestant leader John Knox (c. 1514–72) and containing factions until she made an unwise marriage in 1565. Subsequently her rule fell apart and the nobility forced her out. Exiled and imprisoned in England, she was decapitated there as a traitor in 1587, all her possessions burned. Mary was a woman of extraordinary political talents and immense personal courage, a lover of life as much as a conscientious and charismatic queen, who should be judged not by her failure to bring stability to her fatally unstable country, but by her many successful attempts to do so. She was defeated not because she could not match her enemies, but because they were so numerous and the problems so intractable.

Mary's reign went against a trend of growing royal power, for under James IV and James V the crown had become much more assertive. Yet then, and for centuries after, Scottish government remained quite different from English. From Anglo-Saxon times, the English crown had used a common law and a national circuit court system to exert close and effective centralized judicial control over local and corporate liberties, as well as levying taxes and waging war on a big scale; its kings issued their own coinage. English government was participatory local government – shire, hundred, borough, and parish – but directly answerable to the king. England's medieval kings were intensely powerful men who sometimes lacked authority.

Scotland's monarchy had great authority and limited power, having to support diversity and bolster existing noble privilege until much later. The Scottish aristocracy saw themselves as co-rulers rather than subjects. Local government prior to the late 17th or the 18th century was the lord's or the burgh's government and, while also largely amateur and participatory, the touch of the centre was light. The first royal coins were issued by David I centuries after their English models, and Scottish weights and measures were not standardized until the 19th century. Late medieval Scotland had become a nation built on the monarchy and buttressed by other pillars such as a separate church, a precociously nationalist school of historical writing, and an emerging but already robust legal system. As a state, it was nothing like England, but much closer to the decentralized power structures that characterized most continental countries.

The Unions of 1603 and 1707

The 16th century saw Wales fully assimilated into English government: shires, boroughs, common law, and parliament. England and Wales became a unitary state, possibly the only one in contemporary Europe: royal and parliamentary authority prevailed throughout the kingdom; there was common law; uniform religion; free internal trade; and a measure of identification with the territory and its institutions – 'nationhood' if not nationalism. In time, the Welsh and the English became socially united too, and only the Welsh language survived as a sign of separation. Scotland shared a monarch with England from 1603, but the Anglo-Scottish Union of 1707, like the Anglo-Irish of 1801, was purely legislative, lacking the thorough political, legal, and institutional integration of Wales. Scotland and England were brought together by dynastic union and constitutional instrument.

Queen Elizabeth I of England (1558–1603) was childless and James VI of Scotland, long her heir-apparent, was crowned James I of England in 1603 with 'silent joye, noe great shouting'. James moved his court from Edinburgh to London. He had aspirations to integrate the countries more fully in law, religion, and government, but they came to nothing: even the crown's prerogative powers (those enjoyed simply by virtue of being a prince) were not the same north and south of the border. James's successor, Charles I, was much less politically astute and found out to his cost that the realms remained very different (see Chapter 2).

The Union of Parliaments attracted no more debate than that of crowns in the south either before or after 1707. The English were satisfied with the deal, which secured the succession to the throne, removed the irritant of an independent Scottish parliament, and gave lasting security. The Scots were far more ambivalent, their competing views appearing in more than 500 pamphlets, sermons, and treatises. On one side was the Duke of Queensberry, the queen's commissioner in Scotland, trumpeting the economic and political benefits of Union; on the other, Lord Belhaven, shuddering at the threat to 'our Ancient Mother CALEDONIA'. Many Scots were indeed suspicious, if for very different reasons. Supporters of the ousted James VII, called 'Jacobites' (from *Jacobus*, the Latin for James), rioted against the legislation about who was to succeed Queen Anne. Radical Protestants for their part baulked at the apparent threat to their independent church and law.

In the 1700s and ever since, some Scots saw Union as a sell-out. Poet Robert Burns (1759–96) famously described the Scottish representatives as a 'parcel of rogues'. In fact, many Scots who engineered Union had been exiled in the Low Countries under the later Stewarts and were staunch and highly principled supporters of the 'Glorious Revolution' of 1688–9, when James VII/II fled his realm and William of Orange and Mary (James's daughter) took over. Men like the earls of Stair, Marchmont, and Leven had been discussing and planning an incorporating Union since 1689, believing (as John Knox had done) that it would protect the Scottish Reformation and fend off the military threat to all Protestants posed by Louis XIV's absolutist monarchy in France. They had a truly 'British' standpoint. Aware of Scotland's dire economic condition during the 1690s, they also hoped for preferential access to the blossoming trade with English colonies, blocked since 1651 by Navigation Acts that owed less to the antagonism of crown or people to the Scots (or the Dutch) than to the powerful, self-interested lobbying of English merchants.

Burns also jibed that the representatives were 'bought and sold for English gold', a reference both to 'interest' or corruption (then a normal way of doing business) and to the £400,000 compensation gained by hard bargaining for losses sustained in a spectacularly disastrous colonial venture at Darien (Panama) in 1699. Scots blamed the English for the failure and they may have been right, though disease and Spanish arms played their part, for Scotland had no navy adequate to protect its mercantile marine.

In the end, the balance of opinion among the political classes was that the Union was a 'fair bargain'. It came into being on 1 May 1707. Scotland got 45 members of parliament (MPs) in the House of Commons and 16 places in the Lords. But if the English hoped to forget about the Scots once more, they were soon disappointed.

Political stability might have been secured in England in 1689, but not in Ireland or Scotland, which saw the very first Jacobite rising seize victory at Killiecrankie (Perths., 1689) then slump to defeat in Ireland and Scotland in 1691. Now seen as a sort of emotive nationalism or a doomed romantic anachronism, post-1689 Jacobitism was a mainstream but elite political and religious movement based on divine-right succession (making the monarch one of God's anointed) and close dynastic loyalty. It was not an independence movement, but an alternative claim to the British throne. The Act of Succession, passed in 1701 to allow the house of Hanover to succeed the heirless Queen Anne (as it did in 1714), came from London, not Edinburgh. Its Scottish equivalent, the tellingly named Act of Security (1704), said only that Anne's successor should be a Protestant of her line. Thus there was nothing to stop James VII's son, the 'Old Pretender' James Edward Stewart (1688–1766), converting to claim his throne as James VIII, and then reverting to Catholicism.

For decades, regime change was a live issue and, at times, a real possibility. An attempt by the Old Pretender to land at Edinburgh in 1708 was driven off, but, inspired by divine-right visions and by discontent at the Hanoverian succession, supporters of the Stewarts rebelled in 1715 and provoked a rising in northern England. More people supported the Jacobites than during their next major rising in 1745, but in England they were poorly led and badly organized, making them easy to crush.

Recriminations after the 1715 failure took decades to fade, weakening the Jacobite impetus. Yet by 1745, strong forces destabilized Britain: general antagonism to 30 years of Whig (left-wing) rule among disaffected Tories (as the right-leaning tendency in politics was then known), especially their religious policies; economic woes in Scotland after the Union failed to deliver in the short term; the serious 'Porteous riots' in Edinburgh in 1736; discrimination and destitution in Ireland. In addition, the 1745 Jacobites had important advantages: James Edward's son, Charles Edward Stewart (aka 'the Young Pretender', or 'Bonnie Prince Charlie') was a charismatic leader; he had French and Irish support; his fast, manoeuvrable army seized Edinburgh and in September 1745 he trounced English forces at Prestonpans (East Lothian) in just 15 minutes, moving swiftly south to Derby – just 130 miles from London.

Thereafter the rebels lost the initiative and things started to go wrong. Promises of support from some English Tories were hot air, and military disagreements led to retreat and failure to link up with the French; though even in January 1746 all was not lost, for the Jacobites were still winning victories. Then they retreated into the Highlands which, far from their natural stronghold, deprived them of support from the north-east Lowlands, which in its religious, political, and social makeup was far more sympathetic.

Relentlessly the Hanoverians closed in, amassing troops, money, and supplies while using the navy to isolate the Jacobites. Yet, defeat was still by no means certain when George II's youngest son, the Duke of Cumberland, surprised a depleted force outside Inverness. Judicious use of infantry and artillery broke the rebel charge and in an hour left a third of them dead. The last battle on British soil, Culloden showed the divisions in British society. The field was not coloured tartan versus redcoat, but had multiple hues (and tongues), with half the Hanoverian army Scots. The Pretender fielded an international force of French (always meant to be the backbone), Irish, and English, as well as Scots from Highlands and Lowlands alike.

Defeat at Culloden, driven home by the subsequent scorched-earth policy of Cumberland, irretrievably damaged the Jacobite cause. Charles escaped to live out his days as an Italian drunk, dying in 1788. In the meantime, the defeat of a French invasion fleet in 1759 and Britain's total victory in the Seven Years War (1756–63) killed off the effective threat of regime change, but the government still thought it wise to build the imposing Fort George outside Inverness (1769). The Union was secure and, although people were unsure how to take George I, the Hanoverians were positively adored by the time George III died in 1820.

During George III's reign, a British flag was created to signal Union. James VI/I tried and failed to marry the crosses of St George and St Andrew. The 'Union Jack' originated in the 1650s when the English under Oliver Cromwell really did subjugate the Scots and Irish by arms (it had an Irish harp at its centre), but the present Union flag dates from the Union with Ireland in 1801, when the red saltire of St Patrick was placed within the white diagonal cross of St Andrew. The Lion Rampant is properly a heraldic symbol of the kings of Scotland – a fitting national flag in view of the historic role the monarchy played in making Scotland and keeping it independent.

By 1801, the massively positive material effects of Union had long been plain. Scotland had economic access to England and English colonies, promoting urban development and both agricultural and industrial revolution. For England, where the Union was much more sought after, it offered short-term political security, only consolidated in the longer run by the defeat of Jacobite challenges. For Britain, Union aided the development of empire and economy, which together created the reality of a United Kingdom and made it *the* European power 1763–90 and *the* world power after 1815. But it also left a legacy of resentment and tension between the component countries and within Scotland itself.

Socially and culturally, the gap between Highland and Lowland that had originated in the 14th century (see Chapter 4) was widened by the identification of the Lowlands with 'civilized' values and the Highlanders with 'barbarism'. Politically too, the implications for Scotland were unclear. Englishman and pro-Union spy Daniel Defoe wrote in his *A tour thro' the whole island of Great Britain* (1724–7) that Union had secured Scotland's peace and helped its commerce,

> But I cannot say she has raised her figure in the world at all since that time, I mean as a body. She was before considered as a nation, now she appears no more but as a province, or at best a dominion.

Indeed, the Union created as many questions as it resolved. One lingering argument was over militia and the right to bear arms, which disappeared with Union. For decades, Scots fought in parliament to have both restored – to the respectable at least.

They failed, largely because significant portions of the population were manifestly disloyal to the post-1714 regime, though along the way they raised important points: had the Scottish parliament been merged with, grafted onto, or dissolved into the English; was the Union egalitarian or colonial; did Scots have the rights constitutionally accorded to Englishmen; did they have any rights? American colonists had the luxury of ignoring such issues until the 1760s, but the Scottish background must have been very obvious and it informed not only Revolutionary debates, but also the Second Amendment to the US Constitution (the right to bear arms).

Scots law

Scotland's separate parliament was merged with England's in 1707, but its institutions of education, local government, private law, and religion were preserved. These included establishments which allowed opinion to be articulated and decisions to be reached on a wide range of economic, social, and political issues. The most important arenas were Scotland's principal law courts.

From the writings of distinguished jurists like Balfour, Craig, and Skene, Scots were well aware that their law was distinctive around the Union of the crowns and they were reminded by the first of the great 'institutional' or codifying writers, Viscount Stair, in 1681. Scots consciously based their national identity on their law, especially in the 18th and 19th centuries. It was not a colonial imposition, as it was to the Irish, but an indigenous development, albeit influenced by continental and English traditions. Scots adapted and adopted English legal ideas in the Middle Ages. Scotland had a 'common law' – which could be variously understood as a *ius commune*, or simply the king's law that applied to everyone unless he said otherwise – but not like that of England. Indeed, the main Renaissance influence was French, manifested in the creation of 'estates' (representative components) of parliament, the establishment of the College of Justice in 1532

(Court of Session), and the education and professionalization of lawyers.

Based on a 15th-century judicial committee, the Lords of Council, the Court of Session became the supreme civil court by 1560 and, with a judiciary more secure than in England, a semi-independent, quasi-political body by 1600. Court of Session judges were (and still are) honorific 'Lords'. This political as well as judicial role expanded in the 17th century and was consolidated in the 18th, when the Court of Session can be regarded as one of several substitutes for a parliament. The others were the Convention of the Royal Burghs, declining in importance even before 1707, but not abolished until 1975, and the General Assembly of the Church of Scotland (the 'Kirk'), a major annual event whose social and religious pronouncements, or 'deliverances', were widely reported and which had until the 1980s considerable political impact.

While the Court of Session had influence after the Union the House of Lords acted increasingly as an appellate court: by the 1790s, more than one-third of this type of business came from Scotland. Reform of the Court of Session in 1808 – splitting it and introducing civil jury trial – marked a significant change in Scots law. Previously understood as part of the law of nature and of nations, it became largely self-contained. When it came to social policy (including poor relief and labour relations), judge-made law of the Court of Session was as important as parliamentary statute.

Until the 18th century, the highly devolved Scottish state had extensively delegated criminal justice, even if the components operated together to enforce order in the monarch's name. Royal criminal justice was not fully extended into the localities until the Justiciary Court was reformed in 1672 and centrally supervised circuit courts established in 1708. Until the Heritable Jurisdictions Act came into force in 1748, franchise courts (public jurisdictions in private hands) were common in Scotland. Charters granted some feudal lords 'baronies' or 'regalities' (the latter like English palatinates), each with specified judicial rights, which in the case of regalities extended to all but the most serious crimes reserved for royal courts. Baron courts survived 1748, their limited functions gradually fading away, but they were only abolished in 1948.

Scotland's legal system differed from that of England in almost every regard. Confusingly, legal and administrative officials and bodies with shared names sometimes had different functions and fortunes. From their introduction in 1609 until very recently, Scottish Justices of the Peace were more concerned with administrative matters than judicial; Scotland had coroners, but they did not investigate sudden deaths like their English counterparts; the Scottish Exchequer arrived later and was always a smaller and more limited judicial body than its mighty English equivalent. Nevertheless, legal ways of thinking permeated social relationships and activities much more than in the present day, and law was a more obvious part of the fabric of everyday life. Much of what we would regard as local government was handled by the courts.

English Sheriffs declined to largely honorific status from the 16th century as their Scots equivalent grew in judicial and administrative importance. Established nationwide in the 13th century, they were extensively reformed in 1748. They, or more properly 'Sheriffs-Depute', are not only important local agents of central government, but also the mainstay of the modern judiciary. Sheriff Courts have civil jurisdiction (unless given by statute to another court), distinguishing them from English County Courts (introduced in 1847).

Medieval criminal justice was more about kin and compensation than crime itself, but from the 16th century Scotland had public prosecutors called 'procurators-fiscal' to aid victims or stand in for the crown. The English relied until the 19th century on private prosecutions. Even when professional police were introduced in the 19th century, the Scottish criminal justice system, like many continental countries, remained in the hands of lawyers. Scottish police only collect information and all subsequent action is undertaken by a lawyer in the public service. Modern Scotland's criminal justice is centred on the Lord Advocate, who supervises procurators-fiscal serving in 49 Sheriff-Court districts and 6 sheriffdoms. The High Court of Justiciary is Scotland's supreme criminal court. Nomenclature differs here as well: for example, manslaughter is known in Scotland as 'culpable homicide'.

Aspects of Scotland's historic criminal law look more humane than English, but this comes from the internal dynamic of the law rather than from some vague national characteristic, for law is a social fact that shapes how people think and behave. For example, imprisonment for debt was less stringently enforced in historic Scotland than was notorious in Dickensian England, because it came at the end of the process of bankruptcy or 'insolvency', not its beginning, as creditors had to pay towards support, and because the debtor could seek release by giving up his assets to trustees for his creditors. Mounting a criminal prosecution where foul play was suspected was expensive because it was harder to secure a conviction. Fines and costs were preferred punishments for many offences where other judicial systems might have used corporal sanctions or imprisonment.

Stringent standards of proof meant that one witness was insufficient to secure conviction. This explains Scotland's persistently low rates of prosecution, conviction, and execution (and transportation pre-1857) prior to the abolition of capital punishment in Britain in 1965. The execution rate per head of population during the 19th century was nearly three times higher in England, Wales, and Ireland than in Scotland. The last public hanging in Scotland was at Dumfries in 1868 and the last judicial execution at Aberdeen in 1963. Cost considerations too meant that some aspects of criminal investigation were less rigorously pursued. Sudden deaths were less likely to be investigated and the rate of post-mortems in 20th-century Scotland was much lower than in England.

Continuing legal differences are also clear in civil law, notably property transactions. Freehold in the English sense was unusual in Scotland and was the purest form of feudal tenure, held from the crown. Most owner-occupiers were called 'feuars', a feu or fee farm being a perpetual lease granted in exchange for a large fixed sum and (usually much smaller) subsequent annual payments. Until 2004, most homeowners still had to pay an annual 'feu duty'. Flats or apartments in England are mostly leasehold because someone has to own the ground rent; in Scotland a flat has the same ownership standing as a house. Binding contracts in Scottish property transactions are exchanged between lawyers acting for the parties at a much earlier stage than in England.

The history of making and breaking marriage also differed. After 1753, those under 21 could not marry without parental consent in England. In Scotland, they could (and still can) and Gretna Green (Dumfries.) became synonymous with clandestine marriages, which in Scots law did not require a clergyman or civic official until 1940. All types of marriage conferred the same property rights on Scottish women, though those with property used pre-nuptial agreements more extensively than in England prior to the 19th century. Divorce, which in England required an act of parliament prior to 1858, was more readily available in Scotland. Over time the systems converged, but modern Scottish courts favour 'clean break' settlements and the outcome of divorce proceedings is much easier to predict than in England.

It is often said that English law lent towards providing remedies and learning from precedents, whereas that of Scotland followed the continental civil law tradition in being more concerned with underlying rights or principles (syllogisms) when deciding on particular instances. Yet over time Scots and English law have converged in both theory and practice, showing the continued interplay of legal influences that began in the Middle Ages. In the 20th century, Scots law influenced English solutions as much as vice versa, notably in the English adoption of Scottish ideas of *culpa* (delict) or 'duty of care' in civil suits (1932) and 'diminished responsibility' in criminal trials (1957); the Scots law of marital rape was also exported to England (1991). Legal aid came late to England (1940s) and was based on a modified version of the defence counsel appointed for poor Scots since the 16th century.

Differences remain. Scots lawyers still allow a limited principle of desuetude – laws may fall into disuse because of changes in the overall context of the law – and indeed, Scots law's pervasive flexibility, founded on general understandings of what is right and wrong, is a further source of strength. Mindful of the value of Scottish legal inspiration, those who sat on the important Scottish Law Commission (1964–) sought to harmonize Scotland's laws with others in the United Kingdom rather than to assimilate them to an English model. When the House of Lords recommended England have a new definition of murder in 1989, it found Scotland's to need no tinkering.

Other strengths of the Scottish legal tradition include: the fusion of law and equity (divided in England until the establishment of the High Court in 1873, itself modelled on the Court of Session); the enduring value of 17th- and 18th-century 'institutes' or codifications of law's principles; and the robust body of case law, summarized for the civil law in Morison's *Dictionary of Decisions at the Court of Session* (1811–) and then the 'Session Cases' (1841–), together the nearest equivalent of the *English Reports*. The new frontier is handling European Union law, but Scotland's legal history had made this easier than it is for English common lawyers.

Liberalism, Socialism, and Conservatism

Scotland's pre-1707 parliament had been profoundly undemocratic, 'representative' only in an oligarchic sense. The post-1707 franchise was no different. Scotland in the 18th century was effectively managed, with little interference from London, by a system of aristocratic patronage, making its own place in the British state. An apparent political consensus was created and maintained.

Yet there were many undercurrents of instability. For one thing, differences in the way Scots and English law was implemented undercut the coherence of the British state. In the sphere of religion, Scots were far from ready for early (and apparently enlightened) efforts by the London government to offer Catholics relief from discriminatory legislation. There were 'no popery' riots at Edinburgh and Glasgow in 1779. The vague notion of shared British Protestantism itself sat awkwardly with the deep differences in outlook of its many competing sects – divisions that only widened with recurrent fragmentation of Scottish Presbyterianism in the 18th and 19th centuries (Chapter 2). Religious divisions were as much about different social visions as about theology and church government, signalling a further fissure.

There were political tensions too. Even before mass enfranchisement, local decisions were made and local offices held by members of an informed and concerned local public, whether in a 16th-century rural 'birlaw' court (where adult males made decisions pertaining to farming and the communal good), a 17th-century 'Kirk Session' (like an English select vestry – see Chapter 2), an 18th-century craft incorporation (guild), or a 19th-century social club or trades union. These democratic and participative institutions sat uneasily with oligarchic town councils pre-1833 and with aristocratic power in the counties until it was weakened by franchise reform in the 1860s and after, and by

2. **From remote islands like St Kilda to the major cities, Scots took communal responsibilities seriously**

the creation of representative county councils in 1889. Rapid urbanization too outdated political structures designed for an overwhelmingly rural society with towns of a few hundred people.

Until 1832, Scotland's parliamentary franchise was far more restricted than in England and this provoked a rising tide of middle-class protest. The Scottish electorate was 0.2% of the population, compared with 4% in England, and the burgh franchise was confined to co-opted town councils: Edinburgh's MP at the British parliament in London was elected by just 33 men. The 1832 Reform Act revolutionized the Scottish franchise. The electorate in England increased by 80% from the pre-1832 figure, but in Scotland the change was 1,400%, with 13% of Scotland's adult male population then enfranchised. By 1867, the proportion of males able to vote was approximately equal in Scotland and England at about one-third, and in 1884 the franchise was homogenized across Britain. Yet live-in servants and sons, soldiers in barracks, and those who did not pay rates had no vote: 'no representation without taxation'. In all, 40% of adult males were still unregistered in 1911. Women had to wait until 1918 before they too could vote.

Convergence in the franchise disguises the parallel but quite distinct political histories of Scotland and England. Notable is the enduring strength in Scotland of Liberalism from 1832 to 1914, epitomized in British Prime Minister Gladstone's Midlothian Campaign speeches (1879); England was more consistently Conservative. Liberalism came out of the Protestant, constitutionalist, legalist political tendency that had started in the late 17th century as 'Whig'. Its 19th-century political keynotes were democracy, egalitarianism, and nationalism, but it also stood for free trade, self-help, temperance, and improvement through education.

Additionally, the Union of 1707 allowed for Scottish control over major social establishments: the law, the church, and education. These peculiarly Scottish institutions provided a continuing basis for dual allegiances within a 'unionist nationalism' that was strengthened by making the Lord Advocate responsible for Scottish legislation between 1832 and 1885, when the job passed to the re-instituted Secretary for Scotland. The founding of the Scottish Office in 1885 offered an administratively devolved solution to resurgent nationalist feeling, channelling it into existing British political structures and a Unionist framework. Developing considerable power, the head of the Scottish Office was upgraded to 'Secretary of State for Scotland' with Cabinet status in 1926, a post that reached its apogee with Tom Johnston (1941–5), a politician of great vision and ability who established the North of Scotland Hydro-Electric Board in 1943 and persuaded Churchill to create a Scottish Council of State and a Council of Industry. In his time, the Beveridge Report (1942) committed Britain to a welfare state. Prior to 1999, the Scottish Office supervised most government departments in Scotland and most of its functions are now exercised by the Scottish Executive.

Local government too was greatly altered in the 19th century, allowing more direct participation by more voters. Reformed burgh councils (1833) acted as a focus of local and regional independence. In Scotland's cities, local government was made up of private citizens elected by their peers to part-time, fixed-term public positions in which they were directly responsible to fellow residents. Cities were governed by uniquely Scottish 'police commissions' of 18 to 36 economically independent men, which had tax-raising powers and which dealt with a wider remit of environment, health, and order than what is now described as 'police' (constabulary). 'Police' in the 19th century really meant 'social policy', covering health, roads, cleansing, lighting, sewage (including the provision of public conveniences), water and gas, slaughterhouses, and a fire service – to name but a few – all supervised by local Sheriffs-Depute.

Diverse local publics conducted vigorous debates about local government in 19th-century Scotland as part of widespread participation in civil society. Seen as the arena of optional, collective action around shared values and ends, civil society possesses many spaces, actors, and institutional forms, varying in their degree of formality, autonomy, and power, which mediate between 'public' and 'private', between state and family. Within civil society there was a shared acknowledgement of the legitimate claims of all its members as individuals and groups. The basis lay in Christian charity, understood as mutual regard or amity and peace rather than simple benevolence. Onto this were grafted Renaissance ideas of civic humanism that also stressed shared obligations in pursuit of a 'common wealth'.

Part of the reason for the importance of civil society is that Scotland lacked a 'state tradition' like England's, its people deeply rooted in voluntarism and unused, even in the 19th century, to rule by bureaucrats closely controlled by central government. More than in England, the political system depended on local magistrates and representatives, with administrators who answered locally more than centrally. Policy was made from the bottom up by figures like urban Medical Officers of Health, who enjoyed considerable independent powers, yet whose work was firmly based on an ethos of public service. Even before reform of county government in 1889, there were opportunities for lay participation in important decision making, notably in the elected school boards created in 1873, and membership of the education authorities that succeeded them from 1918–29 included women for the first time.

Scotland's civil society traditionally had fiscal mechanisms to realize its goals. Burghs were financially flexible, empowered to respond to changing needs by legislation enabling them to charge additional levies on, for example, the sale of beer. Acts hypothecated the taxation to specified ends: Greenock built its new harbour in the mid-18th century using beer money and Edinburgh, among other things, to build churches and to fund its university's chair of law. Many towns too had corporate endowments and incomes, known as the 'Common Good', which they were legally obliged to use on collective necessities. This delivered a social dividend in the promotion of a wide spectrum of both private activities and public interests ranging from clubs and welfare projects to civic histories and buildings. The importance of family, community, and locality that this focus implied is preserved in gravestone inscriptions from across 18th- and 19th-century Scotland.

The essentially local focus to political and social life is also clear in British lawmaking on Scotland. After the Union, legislation had to be designated '(Scotland)' before 'Act' or it did not apply there. The total volume of Scottish legislation dropped by 85% after 1707, though local legislation declined by only 30%, showing that Scotland's representatives used their time on issues affecting particular towns or districts – and kept distinctively Scottish law and religion out of the British parliament. Only in the field of economic policy did they continue attempts by the Scottish parliament to foster national growth: for example, protection and bounties for the linen industry from the 1740s.

Much political activity was local, but there were national developments too. Though early 19th-century political change was driven by the middle classes, working people became more coherently political over the century. A tradition of working-class self-help that saw, for example, the Cooperative Women's Guild founded in 1892, crystallized in the formation of organized political parties. James Keir Hardie, a miner, founded the Scottish Labour Party in 1888, which merged with the English Independent Labour Party in 1893. Helped by franchise reform and Liberalism fatally divided over Ireland, 29 Labour MPs were elected for Scotland in 1922 (of 72 Scottish seats) and James Ramsay MacDonald from Lossiemouth (Morays.) became Britain's first Labour Prime Minister, in 1924. He tried to make his party more moderate and acceptable to a middle class frightened by the emergence of focused working-class politics, heading a neo-Conservative administration 1929–35, but was expelled from his party in 1931.

The 1922 successes helped give Scotland a name for socialism, but this was simply one late version of an older Scottish radical tradition. The 19th-century political complexion was Whig or, from c. 1859, Liberal, and the Labour Party came out of ethical, left-wing Liberalism rather than Marxism. These radical ideas are conventionally attributed to the influence of the American and French Revolutions and were signalled in 1790s, 1820s, and 1840s radicalism. In fact, working-class protest and broader theories of resistance to unjust rule, deriving from both secular ideas and religious egalitarianism, long predated these modern revolutions. Scottish ideas informed the world's great revolutions.

Organized labour stood out against capitalistic exploitation and poor living standards, with Glasgow people mounting successful Rent Strikes during World War I. However, true socialists like

John MacLean, Marxist opponent of the war and apparent promoter of a Bolshevik revolution in Glasgow, were less important in their day than as later icons. Indeed, a left-leaning tradition represents the mainstream in modern Scottish politics better than, for example, the truly 'red' Scottish Socialist Party.

Whatever its reputation for socialism and bad industrial relations, 20th-century Scotland was as much Conservative and Unionist, a link created in 1886 when Liberal Unionists split from mainstream Liberals to ally with Conservatives over Gladstone's unsuccessful attempt to promote Irish Home Rule (devolved self-government within the UK). Indeed, Unionism dominated 20th-century Scottish politics, rooted in long-established and deeply felt loyalty to empire and the houses of Hanover and Wettin or Saxe-Coburg-Gotha (which changed its name to Windsor in 1917). Conservatives won a majority of Scottish seats in the first general election of the 20th century on a tide of Boer War patriotism; between 1910 and 1918, they increased their Scottish seats from 7 to 32. During the 1920s, the Liberals faded badly, creating the two-party system (Conservative/Labour) that dominated 20th-century British politics.

The Conservatives had 36 Scottish seats in 1910 and 1955, when they got more than half the Scottish vote (they did less well in between), and only began a secular decline with the growth of nationalism in the 1960s and 1970s and then the emergence of a refocused, rebranded Labour Party ('New Labour') in the 1990s. The fastest rate of electoral decline was during Edward Heath's premiership (1970–4), for as well as presiding over severe economic problems, Heath seemed to personify the unfortunate blend of patronizing arrogance and blithe indifference that Scots long felt the English showed them. Yet it was the years of Margaret Thatcher (1979–90) and John Major (1990–7) that killed support for Conservatism in Scotland all but stone dead. The electorate started dismantling it in 1987, and by the 1997 general election Scotland (and Wales) returned not a

3. Scotland has had a reputation for left-wing politics since the Victorian era

single Conservative MP. In 2008, only one of 59 MPs for Scotland was Conservative.

Nationalism

Scottish Conservatives have since 1965 formally been called 'The Scottish Conservative and Unionist Party'. Behind lip-service to Scottish nationalism, Labour too favoured Union, explicitly so after 1958, and the driving force behind modern devolution has been the Scottish National Party or SNP (so called from 1934). Originating as the National Party of Scotland in 1928, it helped to get the Scottish Office relocated to St Andrew's House, Edinburgh, in 1939, but that was an empty gesture by Unionists and the SNP's first major success was winning the parliamentary seat of Hamilton from Labour in 1967. During the 1970s, it became an important force, taking Glasgow Govan in 1973 and winning one-third of the vote in the 1974 general election by making the acute problems of international capitalism into nationalist issues. To the failure of Upper Clyde Shipbuilders and the fallout from the 1973–4 oil crisis, the SNP added the emotive issue of who benefited from the newly exploited oil riches of the North Sea (Texas more than Scotland, as it turned out).

SNP presence kept the London government on its toes, securing funding for social infrastructure and employment projects (spending on Scotland was 20% higher than the UK average), yet it failed to deliver independence, partly thanks to a referendum loaded by the Labour government in 1979. The terms stipulated that 40% of the total electorate had to vote 'yes' – hardly likely when few 20th-century British governments had been elected by that many.

Scottish devolution happened in 1999 for both negative and positive reasons. There was a reaction against the social and economic policies associated with Margaret Thatcher and John Major. The hugely divisive miners' strike of 1984 deeply alienated Scots. This was compounded by the disastrous community charge or 'poll tax' experiment, introduced a year earlier in Scotland than England (1988) at the instigation of the Tory Scottish Secretary, George Younger. Scots felt their assets were being stripped: not just oil, but flagship companies like United Distillers, taken over in murky circumstances by Guinness in 1986.

Real open-market capitalism razed what remained of Scottish industry, leading to 15% unemployment and many high-profile collapses – steel at Gartcosh, car-making at Linwood, aluminium at Invergordon – while major employers like British Gas and British Telecom slashed jobs. Faith in the state waned and people came to recognize that it was best to deal directly with multi-national capital – and the increasingly important European Economic Community (now the EU), as the Irish were doing.

But there was principle involved too. Scottish support for the Conservatives grew at the 1979 general election, as people wanted stability – prosperity too, and they were as happy as the English to buy their council houses – but 'New Right' Conservatism went head-on with the ethical, socially democratic ideals that had underlain Scottish society for centuries. Using long-established voluntary associations bolstered by the electronic information and communications revolutions, Scots rediscovered their civil society. It is these ideals and associations that currently underpin the success of Scottish devolution.

On 1 July 1999, the Scottish parliament demerged – or perhaps resumed or re-opened in some opinions. In the half century before it was subsumed in 1707, it produced two-thirds of all legislation in Britain, but three-quarters of the acts were 'private'. Scots valued their pre-1707 parliament, an assembly that mediated between the crown and certain vested sectional interests (prelates, royal burgh commissioners, and nobility, for there was no second chamber). Yet it was never to them what the London parliament was to the English: the pulse of the nation's being and a prized guardian of the interests of all. The idea that customary rights and parliamentary sovereignty constrained lords and kings and thus protected 'liberty' had a profound constitutional dimension for the English and was at the heart of documents like Magna Carta (1215), the Petition of Right (1628), and the Bill of Rights (1689).

With nothing like as insistent and intrusive a crown, Scots had had no need for a Magna Carta, even if Alexander II lent his support to the northern English barons who pressed for restraints on the crown, and even if the charter's protections were extended to the Scots (in its statute version it did not apply to Wales or Scotland). And in the Declaration of Arbroath is a dark hint that, should the king fail to protect his subjects, they could legitimately depose him in favour of a better defender and, before and after this, guardians of the realm could legitimately stand in for weak kings, even adults. William Wallace was a guardian. Later the Scots nobility, underpinned partly by such ancient ideas of power-sharing to maintain good governance and partly by more modern religious ones of resistance to tyrants, showed how ruthless they could be in sidelining those who displeased them – like Mary, Charles I, and (for a time) Charles II (see Chapter 2).

In fact, the modern parliament with which Scotland is furnished (and of which it is so justifiably proud) is a reproduction in the English style rather than a restoration of an antique – and better for it, showing how three centuries of Union have changed how Scots think of representation. Yet Scotland's parliament has only one chamber, as it did pre-1707, and it also demonstrates the power of creative adaptation by using European proportional representation rather than the first-past-the-post British parliamentary system when electing members. Its tone is more intimate, informal, and constructively confrontational than the bear pit at Westminster (as the British parliament is usually called).

Today, fewer than two-fifths of voters support independence and pro-Union parties are numerically ascendant at Westminster and at Holyrood (the new Scottish parliament building in Edinburgh is next to the medieval royal palace of that name). Only 7 of 59 Scottish MPs at Westminster are SNP. Yet independence is not a dead issue. Scotland in 2008 has an SNP First Minister, Alex Salmond (the title of Prime Minister is reserved for the United Kingdom), and 47 of 129 MSPs (members of the Scottish parliament) are SNP. The SNP presently espouses a mature, reflective, constructive, and broadly based civic nationalism, mercifully removed from the tartan tub-thumping of the 1970s, when much of its support was a protest vote. It may be a good thing that devolution did not go ahead in 1979 for the atmosphere was far more negative, and perhaps less realistic, than two decades later.

4. The re-opening of the Scottish Parliament, 1999. Looking east, we see the procession up Edinburgh's High Street

Since 1975 local government's corporate voice has been the 'Convention of Scottish Local Authorities' or COSLA, speaking for 1,222 elected representatives in 32 local authorities. Institutions of civil society also offer channels for representation and participation in political as well as social and cultural processes: most important are the Church of Scotland, the Scottish Trades Unions Congress, and the Scottish Council for Voluntary Organisations.

Modern Scotland is *not* fully independent. The Scottish Executive makes and implements policy on 'devolved matters' like economy, environment, housing, transport, and law and order, issues on which the Scottish Parliament can make laws. However, Parliament can only debate, but not legislate on, 'reserved matters' like defence or any aspect of foreign policy, including formal relationships with the EU. These are for Westminster alone.

One important anomaly remains. Scotland is represented twice in the UK, by MSPs at Holyrood and MPs at Westminster (as well as 7 MEPs in Europe). This is a compromise necessary to maintain Union, but unpopular with the English, who resent Scots MPs voting on issues that affect only England, while their English counterparts cannot vote on the same matters in Scotland. Some English also complain that they subsidize Scotland, despite the problems in identifying who generates wealth and who owns resources. Better than bickering over where money comes from is to look at the uses to which it is put, where the Scottish parliament's policies on healthcare and education (among others) offer a fine example.

Chapter 2
Religion

Pre-Christian belief

Christianity probably came to Scotland with the Romans in the 2nd century AD, but it did not enter a spiritual vacuum. Standing stones like those at Callanish (Lewis) or the chambered tomb of Maes Howe (Orkney), both dating to the time of the pyramids of Egypt (c. 3000–2000 BC), show a sophisticated society that could organize labour, extract surplus to support religious and secular elites, and mount elaborate (if now obscure) rituals based on mathematically precise astronomical alignments. The landscape of southern and eastern Scotland is full of lesser 'barrow' (earth) or 'cairn' (stone) burials that suggest a reverence for ancestors and possibly also acted as markers of family or tribal lands. More humbly, the drink-filled beakers buried with the dead similarly suggest that Stone Age people had a view of the afterlife and thus a religion; they also started burying people individually c. 2500 BC. Mummified and manipulated Bronze Age bodies on South Uist (Outer Hebrides) also show awareness of an afterlife and a highly developed notion of ancestry. Iron Age people saw metalworking as supernatural, blended with offerings, feasting, and possibly also human sacrifice as an aid to prophecy (Minehowe, Orkney). How they saw religion affecting the living is unclear, for most of what is known of life comes from the more permanent monuments to and observances surrounding the dead, though standing stones, fire pits, and occasional findings of fertility symbols suggest concern with cycles of regeneration.

The early church

The spread of Christianity from the Lowland Britons and the Irish Scots to the Picts, begun by shadowy missionaries in the early 5th century, was continued by the more certain figure of St Columba (6th century). One thing that is clear from the intricately carved, if mysterious, Pictish standing stones of c. 700 to c. 900, found from Strathearn (Perths.) up the east coast to Caithness, is that they represent not secular imagery or pagan idolatry, but a rendition of Christian symbols derived from texts and illuminated manuscripts. Sophisticated in realization and full of meaning, these stones (and metalwork in the same style) mark the integration of the Picts into mainstream Christian Europe. They manifested a powerful visual theology most famously exemplified in the Lindisfarne Gospels of c. 700, showing the rich mixture of Celtic, Anglo-Saxon, and Roman elements of Northumbrian Christianity; the Irish Book of Kells (c. 800); and the 10th-century Book of Deer, an illuminated gospel compiled on an Irish model by monks at Deer (Aberdeens.; founded c. 600) with later Gaelic marginalia.

Yet even within Augustine's vision of a universal church, there were distinct branches from the 7th century, marked among other things by bitter disputes over the date of Easter. Scotland was initially linked to St Columba then to St Peter in the 8th century, thanks to a closer association with Northumbria. Ultimately, Celtic Christianity was more influential than Roman with the success of St Andrew from the 9th century. After the Synod of Whitby (664), Northumbria tended towards St Peter, patron saint of the archbishopric of York. The association between St Cuthbert, Lindisfarne, and the West Saxon kings was cemented by the establishment of a shrine at Durham in 995, which gave a potent religious meaning to 'English' rule that was reinforced by lavish

5. This outstanding 'high cross' on Islay, topped by a virgin and child, represents a fusion of the different types of Christianity found across northern Britain and Ireland

gifts of land and privileges to the bishop of what became the Palatinate of Durham. With defeat at Carham (1018), both the religious and political focus of Northumbria shifted south.

(Saint) Margaret, Malcolm III's English wife and a political heavyweight in her own right (d. 1093; canonized 1251), helped further to homogenize Scottish religious practices and extend ecclesiastical administration. Parishes emerged from c. 1100, and long before there was a 'state', there was a Church hierarchy and government that helped to unify Scotland, albeit within a supra-national Church. It was not until the reign of James VI that civil bureaucracy equalled ecclesiastical. A British (or even pan-European) religious identity coalesced around the flourishing monastic tradition begun in Scotland by Columba, though important early monasteries like Dunkeld were usually royal foundations (unlike Ireland). Monastic growth in alliance with secular powers culminated in the great Benedictine and Cistercian abbeys that spread as far north as Kinloss and Pluscarden (Morays.) and as far west as Iona in the 12th century, mighty institutions with political, economic, administrative, and cultural significance as well as religious. Again, two-thirds were crown foundations: like contemporary castles, they were handles used to possess regions. From 1192, the papacy supported the independence of the Scottish Church (its 'special daughter') when Welsh dioceses were still dependent on Canterbury.

Kings, aristocracies, and senior churchmen were closely allied (sometimes kin), trading political protection and advancement of a cult for spiritual legitimation of a ruler. St Andrew's was a minority cult, possibly imported from the Northumbrian monastic centre at Hexham to St Andrews (Fife) before being promoted to near-national status by a 9th-century Pictish king, a development commemorated in the 'Forteviot Arch' from the ancient Pictish capital in Perthshire. Ancient churches stood or fell as royal churches, and between c. 800 and 1100 their economic needs were subordinated to kings who had to combat the Norsemen. Yet the bond survived. In the 12th century, the crown supported the church over the collection of tithes from often reluctant laymen. Over time, monarchs continued the successful alliance with the Church, begun in the Dark Ages, by identifying themselves with regional saints like Ninian (Galloway) or Duthac (Ross), a process that enhanced their national authority and legitimacy while also signalling a respect for provincial interests that lay at the heart of political achievements.

Medieval Catholicism

Late medieval religion was comfortable blending elements of Christianity and paganism in a rich visual tapestry. The astonishing 15th-century Roslin, or Rosslyn, chapel (a 'collegiate' church, founded by the powerful Sinclair family, in Midlothian) is festooned with carvings that range from conventional depictions like the crucifixion or the seven virtues and deadly sins to more surprising images that include multiple representations of the 'green man', a pagan fertility symbol, and even an angel playing the bagpipes. Belief in spirits was a part of popular religion. Following Celtic tradition, Scottish fairies could be male or female (English were always female) and they had no monarch. Fairy beliefs were often linked to marginal or dangerous features of the landscape, and the Loch Ness 'monster' is simply an example of a malignant water spirit, or 'kelpie', eager to drag people into its abode. The association with a corporeal aquatic creature originated in a 1933 newspaper report that caught the English imagination and, discreetly managed, blossomed into an enduring tourist generator.

Celtic veneration of water was given sanction by early Christian missionaries who blessed 'holy' wells and springs, of which there were more than 600 on the eve of the Reformation. Christianity flourished in Scotland because it dovetailed its message with existing belief systems. Another example is the start of the pre-Christian year, Samhuinn (31 October), turned into a festival of the dead by the early church. Later travellers in the Highlands and Islands wrote of second sight and of the monitory power of dreams.

The late medieval Scottish Church was a successful and resolutely independent part of Christendom. Indeed, the vitality of late medieval religion suggests the Protestant Reformation of 1560 was far from inevitable. There is no evidence that the Scottish Church was any worse than it had been or that it was any less spiritually effective than elsewhere in Europe. On the contrary, it was pious and popular. Evidence of religious vitality includes: collegiate churches like Lincluden (Kirkcudbrights.), remodelled in the early 15th century, and the Magdalen Chapel in Edinburgh's Cowgate (endowed just before the Reformation); confraternities (often the worshipping arm of the new urban craft incorporations of the Renaissance – like the metalworkers who took over the Magdalen Chapel); pilgrimages; and dramaturgy. Support for heretics (opponents of Church teachings) was minimal and effectively suppressed.

There were undeniably structural problems with the late medieval Church in Scotland: its wealth was channelled into noble pockets or those of the clerical elite; funds that might have gone to boost parochial services went instead towards building lavish chapels for the upper classes; monasteries were usually presided over by 'commendators', or non-monastic sons of the nobility. Yet these were not the reasons for the Reformation. Resembling a large business, the Church had extensive secular involvement and an important political dimension, but that did not necessarily harm its spiritual functions or charitable role. Indeed, most people before 1559 thought that the Catholic Church would regenerate from within – as it had begun to do across Europe since 1545 under the guidance of the Council of Trent (the first Scottish reforming council was in 1549). Yet within a few years, a church that had thrived for a millennium was swept away.

Reformation

Scotland's Protestant Reformation resembled England's in being politically initiated and in only slowly winning the hearts and minds of the people, but there the similarity ends. England's Reformation was made by a strong crown for political (mostly dynastic) reasons. Its theology was a mild, middle-of-the-road, modified Lutheranism, a religion of German origin which stressed salvation through the believer's faith and which was not that distinct from Catholicism.

Scotland's reformed theology was Calvinist, a strict creed born in Geneva (Switzerland) that stressed God's power over salvation and the duties of his people in life. Scotland's Reformation was forged by revolutionary, anti-French Protestant nobles (with English political and military help) and an anglophile Calvinist ministry (Knox himself had long lived in England). Together nobles and pastors took advantage of weakened monarchy to establish a radical Kirk that itself gradually became a potent political force and an active agent of social change.

Changing religious policies in England made its Reformation ebb and flow between c. 1530 and c. 1660, whereas in Scotland the adoption in August 1560 of a Protestant Confession of Faith and the ending of Mass and the authority of the pope was decisive, with radical elements pushing strongly from the outset for Calvinist theology and Presbyterian church-government. Even taking a slightly broader view, the 'political' Reformation was accomplished between 1557 and 1567. However, the search to secure and broaden it had explosive political implications in the longer term.

From exile, Knox was able in the mid-1550s to rally support in areas with Protestant cells (Lothians, Fife, Ayrshire, and Angus) and to make political contacts with sympathetic nobles disaffected by French dominance of Scottish foreign policy and domestic political life. In 1559, his fiery preaching triggered a rebellion against Queen Mary based on a potent mix of Protestantism and patriotism. Yet, against a background of uncertainty and civil war in the 1560s and 1570s, Protestantism spread slowly outside certain towns like Edinburgh, Perth, and St Andrews, and a 'people's Reformation', comprising broadly based acceptance and promotion of Protestantism in countryside as well as town, did not come until the 1620s. By then, James VI/I (Protestant, but a hierarch to the core) had reintroduced bishops (1610). They had been suspended in favour of Presbyterian organization in 1592, but were not abolished and the Kirk remained one of the estates of parliament. Thereafter Kirk Sessions and Presbyteries were established nationwide.

Presbyterian church government is participative (perhaps even democratic) in its organization. Parish Kirk Sessions comprising minister and co-opted lay elders send delegates to Presbyteries who are in turn represented at Synods, with a General Assembly at the top. The head of the Church of England has been the monarch since Henry VIII (1509–47). In contrast, the temporary chair of the Church of Scotland was and is an elected official called the Moderator of the General Assembly. While represented by an observer, the Lord High Commissioner, the monarch has the status of an ordinary member and, if in attendance, comes as an invited guest (though for a time after 1584 royal supremacy was asserted). Prior to 1690, Scottish church organization fluctuated with politics: episcopacy 1584–92, 1610–38, 1661–90, presbytery in between, though bishops and presbyteries co-existed. Politically, the Church of Scotland could not be more different from the Church of England, which classed Presbyterianism as a branch of religious 'Dissent'.

The theology of the reformed Church of Scotland also differed from the tepid Lutheranism of the Tudor Church of England and its crypto-Catholic manifestations under the Stewarts. It was Calvinist in dogma (the English called this tendency in their church 'Puritan'), a more austere set of beliefs marked by simplicity in church furniture and in observances that focused on the ministry of God's Word. Communion, the only sacrament in the Church of Scotland, was taken infrequently and there were many other differences. Scots Calvinists, for example, frowned on funeral services (not officially sanctioned by the Kirk until 1897). Most distinctively, Calvinists believe in predestination: people are born among the elect (who will be saved) or the reprobates (who will be damned); though they cannot know which and cannot alter their destiny, they must strive in their lives to glorify God and to be worthy of his grace.

Socially too Calvinism's impact was different. The received image of post-Reformation Scotland is grim and joyless, with moral discipline and Sabbath enforcement eliminating festivities associated with Christmas, Easter and saints' days. Yet initiatives to keep Sunday special actually originated in the 11th century. Even after the Reformation, popular revelry persisted in the face of official disapproval. The baxters (bakers) of a Calvinist stronghold like Perth continued with the celebration of their patron saint's day; Yuletide (a thoroughly pagan festival) still gave rise to several weeks of merry-making; and the traditional May and midsummer feasting continued into the 1620s, when the elders of the church effectively introduced toleration of these practices in exchange for a fine, which amounted to a tax on entertainment for the benefit of the poor. Austere Calvinist burial observances too were tempered by conventional practices.

In short, the Reformation did not create a 'dour' (dull) land, but accommodated aspects of popular festivities to Calvinist sensibilities in a search to refine faith, discipline, and order. Indeed, like early Christianity, its success depended on compromising with existing forms and beliefs to create a new and diverse Protestant culture of seasonal observances, ritual, costume, festival, and song.

There is a darker side to the triumph of Calvinism, for one way the Kirk established itself was by participating in witch-hunting in the century after c. 1590. The witch craze in Scotland threw up twelve times more executions per capita than in England and only Germany had more intense persecutions. Torture was unusual in Scottish trials and was closely controlled by the central judiciary. Witch hunting was not directly woman hunting, but most accused and executed were female because it was believed they were 'the weaker vessel', more susceptible to the Devil's wiles. The last witch was executed as late as 1727.

Religion and politics after the Reformation

The Kirk's sometimes hesitant and irregular progress was partly because it had to make accommodations with popular attitudes and partly because it depended for its existence on politics. Its early dependence was material. England's Reformation was made by Henry VIII and he got most of the immediate economic and patronage advantage from dissolving the monasteries in the 1530s. James V too exploited the rights the pope gave him to nominate to vacant prelacies and to acquire the assets of six abbeys for his illegitimate sons; he also taxed the church heavily, but went no further. John Knox hoped the spoils of the church would build a reformed commonwealth, but after a Reformation made by nobles ecclesiastical wealth went largely to nobles. Some of their descendants still own former church lands today, when the Church of Scotland is far less significant as a landowner than is the Church of England.

To defend and promote itself, the Kirk formed a powerful, determined, and well-organized lobby set on 'reforming the reformation'. However, it was divided between two wings. One led by intellectual Andrew Melville (1545–1622) was Calvinist, clerical, keen on the 'imposition of godliness', and wary of the crown. James VI's tutor, George Buchanan (1506–82), was another of its leading lights: he thought supreme authority resided not in the king, but in the General Assembly of the Kirk. The other was a state-dominated, anti-clerical, theologically more diffuse wing. All in all, it was a truly radical Reformation. At the time of the Union of the Crowns, some hoped the peoples of Scotland and England would, like the tribes of Israel, 'hold one worship of God, and go up to Jerusalem together', but this was never likely.

The Kirk gradually eroded traditional social relationships by taking on the care of the poor and by creating a network of courts to discipline local communities. The victims in the process were kinship and lordship. The Kirk contributed from the mid-17th century, when its power was at its height, to the developing idea of a public authority in the land. Yet along the way it could just as easily be at odds with secular powers and it was not until 1690 that the Kirk became the Church of Scotland 'by law established'.

One reason why the Kirk sat awkwardly with political establishments lay in the idea of 'covenanting'. Medieval Scots greatly valued the practice of 'bonding', a formal and public compact between men to demonstrate personal and political loyalty. John Knox transferred this into the religious sphere as a 'covenant' or 'league and covenant': a bond or even a contract where God's people upheld his word against all comers in exchange for His grace and salvation. Joining together in these bonds, called covenanting, put participants or 'Covenanters' above conventional worldly authority. It was the most politically radical aspect of the Scottish Reformation, with profound implications for all of Britain.

Just how radical it was became clear in the 1630s. James VI was an outstanding king of Scots and (as James I) a good king of England, managing to contain the implications of the two separate Reformations. Charles I lacked his father's political sense and brought them on a collision course. He went through two coronations, one at Westminster in 1626, another at Holyrood in 1633. The Scots were a bit hazy on what an adult monarch should do at a coronation, not having seen one since 1406. Charles improvised and knelt ceremoniously. An apparently trivial detail, this was a calculated statement about a *British* monarchical church and not some ghastly mistake, for it was reminiscent of the way Anglicans (and strictly also Scots since 1617/18) had to kneel for communion. More, Charles had his bishops decked out in what looked like Catholic vestments and he wore perfume and balm, adding smells to the bells shipped in for the occasion (Calvinists frowned on such sensual trappings).

Squandering what remained of the legacy of loyalty he inherited in 1625, Charles went on to promote bishops' power and a new Prayer Book, while at the same time leaving the political nation anxious about its social and material privileges. Open rebellion began in 1638 and a National Covenant was signed to resist Charles' innovations. Within a year there was a *de facto* aristocratic republic that continued ruthlessly and relentlessly to dismantle royal power. Thus began what are known more broadly as the 'Wars of the Three Kingdoms'. The Scots began Charles' downfall and their covenanting ideas set the tone for armed resistance throughout Britain in the following decade.

The period between 1637–8 and 1651 showed the problems of creating a composite monarchy out of a dynastic agglomerate of England and Wales, Scotland and Ireland, as well as the insuperable difficulties in reconciling Reformations whose trajectories were so different. The Church of England was comprehensive, but necessarily contained compromises and ambiguities. The Kirk aimed to encompass only those who followed its unambiguous line to the letter. The Scottish Revolution forced Anglicans to confront their comfortable accommodations and to recognize their political implications. During the 1640s, nobility and Kirk played the king (as he used them) in an ultimately deadly game that initially sought to protect the Scottish Reformation. Because religious changes were pointless without political structures to secure them, the search for stability ended in a battle for control of Britain.

The Scottish debacle emboldened opponents of Charles' policies in England and he was obliged to call parliament after 11 years of personal rule. After defeat by the Scots and amid mounting disquiet, the king was forced to flee London when rebellion broke out in Ireland in 1641. Military fortunes ebbed and flowed until the decisive defeat of the royalists at Naseby (Northants.) in 1645. Charles, duplicitous as ever, tried to negotiate with the Scottish nobility and royalist Covenanters called 'Engagers', but that alliance too was defeated in 1648. The religious, military, and political histories of Scotland and England (and Ireland) became inextricably entwined during the 1640s and 1650s.

Charles I was executed by the English in 1649 and his son forced to deal with the Scots. After signing the National Covenant and the Solemn League and Covenant framed in 1643, Charles II was crowned at Scone on New Year's Day 1651, provoking Oliver Cromwell to invade Scotland. Cromwell saw himself as a liberator of Scotland, not a conqueror, and his rule is less bitterly remembered by Scots than Irish. In 1654, he created the first truly unitary rule of the British Isles.

If Charles thought anything of the Covenant, he did not show it when returned to the throne in 1660. Aided by Scottish nobility who wanted to repair their power, the Restoration of the monarchy in 1660 brought about more dramatic changes than in England. Presbyterians were humbled politically and one-third of the clergy were expelled in 1662.

Convinced of their righteousness in a way far more dangerous than their English dissenting equivalents, this rump of Covenanters engaged in a fierce conflict with the politico-religious establishment both at home and from exile in the Netherlands.

A reluctant Protestant figurehead, the ninth earl of Argyll, led a rising against James VII/II in 1685. It was fatally weakened by internal divisions, but the Covenanters were eventually able to engineer not the peaceful fudge that was the 'Glorious Revolution' in England, but a violent, vindictive, and partisan reaction that reintroduced Presbyterianism in 1690. So charged was the atmosphere that in 1697 an Edinburgh student called Thomas Aikenhead became the only person in Britain ever to be executed for blasphemy. The 1707 Union notionally protected the position of the Church of Scotland, but within a few years a Scottish Episcopalians Act (1711) effectively circumvented that, passed in flat contradiction of Union guarantees by a Westminster parliament 'high' on High-Church Toryism.

Episcopalianism and Catholicism

Seen by some as another sign the English could not be trusted, the Act's aim was to help Episcopalians, for not all Scots were Presbyterians. Episcopalianism is a hierarchical form of church organization, usually headed by archbishops and bishops, with liturgies and beliefs much closer to Catholicism than to Calvinism. The Episcopalian Church in Scotland is not Anglican, but it has drawn closer to Anglicanism since the 19th century and is now part of their 'Communion', its churches or congregations sometimes controversially termed 'English'. Scottish Episcopalianism is 'high' in doctrine, but 'low' in practice (for long close to Presbyterianism), and there are still clear differences with Anglicanism: for example, archbishops had been introduced in 1472 (St Andrews) and 1492 (Glasgow), but lapsed after 1704. It too had divisions: 18th-century Episcopalians were split between Hanoverians and Jacobites. To this day there remains debate about relations between Scots Episcopalianism and Anglicanism.

The heartland of Episcopalianism was in the north-east Lowlands: another manifestation of how localized and regionalized was Scottish cultural life. Protestantism quickly became a part of being Scottish in the Lowlands, but less so in parts of the Highlands where (as in Ireland) Catholic resurgence eventually created a glass ceiling to block the Protestant missionary effort. Catholic cells existed in some towns and around nobles like the Montgomeries of Eglinton (Ayrs.) and Gordons of Huntly (Aberdeens.) during the early 17th century, but open Romanists by 1800 numbered only about 30,000 in a population of 1.6 million (2%); Episcopalians Comprised 3%.

Modern Scottish Catholicism is not, however, some lingering survival of the Middle Ages. It certainly draws on centuries of indigenous influence, but it owes more to: missionary work in parts of the Highlands and Islands from the late 17th century; 19th-century Irish immigration; regeneration since the emancipation of Catholics from religious, social, and political restrictions in 1829; and the reintroduction of Catholic bishops in 1878. By the 1870s, a coherent Roman Catholicism with a strong cultural identity existed in areas of the Highlands, but its heartland lay in the towns of west-central Scotland and in Dundee and Edinburgh. Catholics were one in twenty of Scotland's population in 1851 and numbered about 550,000 or 11% by 1914.

Victorian legislation enabled denominational education as part of the obligation to provide schooling, an opportunity seized by the Catholic Church to strengthen its institutional and social basis. Catholic schools provided by the Church and by Irish voluntary groups became fully publicly funded in 1918. There are currently 418 Catholic schools in Scotland, accounting for approximately 15% of all publicly funded schools, but educating perhaps 40% of pupils in greater Glasgow. In addition, there are three Episcopalian schools and one Jewish school in the public sector. The 'default' option is not Church of Scotland, for since 1872 state schools have been 'undenominational' and no religion now has legal privilege. Some see faith schools as beacons of educational excellence, others as forces for division in a society seeking reconciliation and shared identity.

Resurgent Catholicism was not without its opponents. Anti-Catholicism had its roots in the Reformation and the European wars of religion that lasted until the end of the 17th century, when great Catholic powers like France and Spain really did try to eradicate Protestantism by force. It was revived as a pan-European tendency in the mid-19th century. On the one hand, nationalist movements eschewed supra-national solidarities and ever-more-powerful governments frowned on the Church's wealth and adherence. On the other Catholics sought actively to protect and promote their faith by exploiting material and cultural resources like education and sporting clubs. Hibernian Football Club was founded in 1875, inspiring in turn Glasgow Celtic FC in 1888 – though both came after Glasgow Rangers FC (1873) and Heart of Midlothian FC (1874). The legacy in parts of Scotland (and in English towns like Liverpool) was chronic sectarian tension.

Division and disruption

For John Knox and his followers, history began at the Reformation, but the history of Protestantism is one of multiple divisions. For a brief period up to the 1630s, competing but overlapping visions of Christian community coalesced into a relatively stable, homogeneous Kirk. Yet, by stressing the individual's relationship to God mediated solely through the Bible and by downplaying hierarchy, Protestantism always contained the seeds of its own fragmentation. Within a century – marked by two major revolutions over religious order and religious faith – the Kirk had begun a series of rifts that produced the most heterogeneous Protestantism anywhere in modern Europe. The post-Union political consensus was based partly on the fiction of unity in religion, yet in reality the history of British Protestantism has been of parallel faiths, not a common one.

At its very moment of triumph in 1690, the Church of Scotland split from Episcopalianism, with which it had co-existed for a century, but even within its own ranks some refused to accept a non-covenanted Church. The next major split came in 1733 with the 'Original Secession', when conservative Covenanters baulked at state influence. The 'Second Secession' of 1761, which saw the creation of the 'Relief Church', was again caused by differences of opinion about how churches should relate to the state and also over lay patronage (appointment of clergy by other than the flock, reintroduced in 1711). In England, nomination of clergymen was overwhelmingly in the hands of individuals. In contrast, Presbyterians expected to choose their own pastor democratically, but after 1711 most rural appointments were in the gift of landowners (the Crown had the right to appoint about one-third of Scotland's parish clergy). Circumspect patrons consulted about appointments, but not all were so tactful.

These rifts created Protestant splinter groups. The Church of Scotland itself divided into 'moderate' and 'evangelical' wings c. 1750–1830 (the latter keeping religion a vital, regenerating force), while the early 19th century saw a further wave of popular religious revival movements. Coupled with this was a broadly based drift away from the established church, once again because of opposition to patronage and secular influence. This ended in the Disruption of 1843 and the establishment of the Free Church of Scotland ('free' from state interference in its internal affairs) by two-fifths of established clergy and one-third of the laity.

Bewildering as it is to follow, the fragmentation of Protestantism actually helped the faith by successively stimulating spirituality. The main splits came at periods when evangelicalism was strong, while more choice also allowed expansion of religious participation. There was a surge in church and school building after the Disruption by the three main Protestant churches: Church of Scotland, Free Church, and United Presbyterian Church, the last founded in 1847 by the union of the United Secession Church (founded in 1820 to encompass the various 18th-century Secession churches), and the Relief Church.

Indeed, religion remained central to everyday life in Victorian Scotland, dominating organized leisure, the formation of social policy, and the moral values of temperance and self-help. Yet there was also a negative effect. Diverging values and widening social differences were fragmenting Highland and Lowland societies in the 18th and 19th centuries. The religious schism of 1843 was linked to emerging class differences, and theological disputes were taken very seriously by Scots in ways hard to imagine today. Disruption also robbed the Church of Scotland of its political claim to represent local communities and made reform of social security (the 'Poor Law') essential (1845). By 1851, three-fifths of churchgoers did not attend Church of Scotland services.

Whatever the effects of fragmentation, Scots clergymen retained considerable independence and social influence. Scotland's established clergy were by the 1620s a tightly knit professional group: better educated, more secure, and better paid (by landowners in rural parishes and burgh councils in the towns) than their English counterparts. Scottish Protestant clergy were called 'ministers', not vicars or rectors and definitely not priests, who had 'charges' not livings, and who lived in 'manses', not rectories. They had to work harder, for parishes were generally much bigger than in England – 900 for 30,000 square miles compared with 11,000 in an area of 50,000 square miles – and they were more closely supervised by presbyteries (62 in number c. 1720).

Nor was the Kirk an agency of the state, but a semi-detached body staffed by staunchly independent ministers. Attempts to create civil rather than simply ecclesiastical parishes on the English model failed (nor were manors ever successfully introduced into Scotland) and there were, for example, no clerical magistrates, who comprised one-third of English JPs c. 1830. The clergy in Scotland *look* a bit like state functionaries, but were in fact purely voluntary agents in secular causes they thought worthwhile: poor relief, social control, and social improvement. For example, they

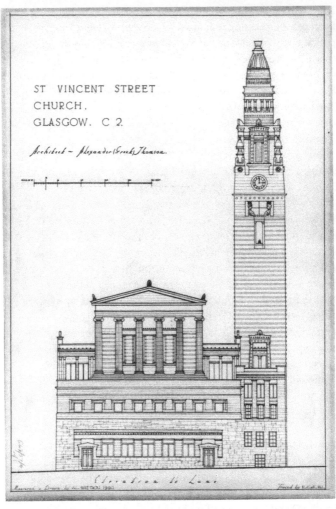

ST VINCENT STREET
CHURCH.
GLASGOW. C 2.

Architect ~ Alexander (Greek) Thomson.

6. St Vincent Street Church, designed by Alexander 'Greek' Thomson, whose strikingly original style exemplifies the religious vitality, wealth, and confidence of Scotland's Victorian cities

served on the boards of lunatic asylums and other public bodies, and compiled information about social life and economic conditions. The first or 'Old' *Statistical Account*, a multi-volume compendium of parish reports published in the 1790s, affords such detailed information and was followed up by a fuller *New Statistical Account* (published by the Kirk, 1834–45). In sharp contrast, most Scottish clergy flatly refused to have anything to do with administering the first census of British population in 1801 as they did not accept its social relevance.

Secularization?

In 1900, Scotland had four main Protestant churches: Church of Scotland, United Presbyterian Church, Free Church, and Episcopal Church. In that year, the second two formed the United Free Church, which in 1929 was reconciled with the Church of Scotland, leaving Episcopalians and some radicals like the Free Presbyterian Church (1893) out on a limb. For all levels of society, church attendance and involvement in religion held up well throughout the 19th century. Half the population were active churchgoers in 1900, and it was not so much the Victorian urbanization (that contemporaries feared made the working classes Godless) as 20th-century bourgeois suburbanization that caused mass secularization. Indeed, church attendance only started to plummet from the 1960s. Now even the Catholic Church has deep concerns about declining vocations and attendance (though still at about one-third), and, like the increasingly ecumenical Anglican Communion, looks to the developing world for personnel and vitality.

Regardless of their nominal faith (40% profess none at all), most modern Scots are best seen as 'diffusive Christians'. Less charitably, the Disruption leader Thomas Chalmers termed them the 'lapsed masses'. They have a genuine sense of involvement with religion, manifested less in the obvious pieties of worship (only one in ten now attends church at least once a month) than in occasional participation in rites of passage and in adherence to moral or civic standards that are inescapably (if not exclusively) Christian. Non-Christian faiths account for a small proportion of modern Scotland's 5.1 million inhabitants – for example, there are 40,000 Muslims and 15,000 Jews, the latter mostly found in Glasgow – and 'alternative', or New Age, spirituality (notably at Findhorn, Morays.) is prominent, but atypical.

The Church in Scotland has had an enduringly bad press that modern agnostics or atheists seize upon. The Kirk must indeed bear its share of blame for the witch-hunting that convulsed Lowland Scotland c. 1590–1690 (and an episode of gay-burning in 1682), though it was building on widespread social and political fear of witchcraft. To us believing in witches seems bizarre, burning them barbaric, but in a world saturated with the supernatural where personal, geographical, and cosmic space were intertwined it made perfect sense. In its heyday too, the Kirk controlled aspects of life modern people see as utterly personal 'human rights', like what courting couples could do. A notable free liver, Robert Burns satirized the intolerance of the Kirk, having suffered at the hands of those he classed as 'the houghmagandie [fornication] pack' of its elders.

The Kirk also controlled what anyone (in or out of church) could do during religious services, though again modern concepts of privacy and individualism date to the 18th century at the earliest. Adultery, for example, seriously disrupted close-knit communities and was regarded as wrong not only by the Kirk, but also by secular authorities (it was a capital offence for a time) and indeed by most people. The Catholic Church also proscribed it and countless other manifestations of human frailty and popular culture. Divorce too, then and now, uprooted lives and often impoverished women.

Church discipline seems alien to us and so too does the Calvinist faith. Modern readers may find it easier to appreciate an apparently animated historic religion like Catholicism, with strong visual, expressive, and performative dimensions to it – a sort of 'reality religion' – and are quick to write off Calvinism as dour, introverted, and self-opinionated. If we believe in Christianity, it is probably in the idea that Jesus died for us all rather than in the devastating selectivity of predestination. But this ignores the inner warmth, hope, and humility attached to evangelicalism and the theology of the elect. Involving ministry, social activism, and a stress on both biblical authority and Christ's suffering, evangelicalism has periodically reinvigorated Christianity. Scotland has been a crucible for such movements since the Reformation.

A particularly austere form of Calvinism exists in parts of the north-east and in the Hebrides, where perhaps a half of the population are still regular churchgoers. Embodied in the Free Church and the ultra-conservative Free Presbyterian Church, of which Ulster's Dr Ian Paisley is a minister, it frowns on religious services at funerals, insists that shops and public houses should be closed on communion days, and is strictly Sabbatarian. Only in 2002 did Sunday flights to and from Stornoway commence, and only in 2006 did the Kirk on the Isle of Lewis first allow Sunday ferries to ply to Ullapool. One can feel on Lewis intense, living religious devotion and also sense the power that the Church once had in mainland Scotland. While seemingly intolerant of personal choice, such manifestations arguably have more dignity and depth than the quasi-religious emotionalism of public involvement in events like funerals of the famous.

There is another side to religion and churches. Modern readers may see religion as a conservative force that is largely about rules and denial – for example, discouraging extra-marital sex (and sex education) and promoting restrictions on Sunday retailing. Yet the church since Christ has been a constructive and often radical force for change. In the Middle Ages, it created clear rules about fundamental social institutions like marriage and inheritance; its much-used courts dealt with these issues and with disputes ranging from defamation of character to debt; at the time of James VI it encouraged an end to blood feud as a way of containing conflict; the late 18th-century drive for smallpox inoculation and vaccination was led by parish clergy; religious evangelicals were in the vanguard of the early 19th-century campaign against slavery; the values of economy, self-denial, and self-sufficiency, that were at the heart of Victorian working- and middle-class movements for improvement, were grounded in Christian morality; social legislation from the Factory Act of 1833 onwards was founded on the charitable ideal of helping those who could not help themselves.

Churches were vigorous supporters of black nationalism in the 1940s and 1950s, they played an active part in discussion both of disarmament and devolution in the 1980s and 1990s, and they now want to 'make poverty history'. Scotland's churches and the faiths on which they are based – all of them – have for centuries provided the moral underpinnings and the organizational structure of much that is good about its society.

Chapter 3
Education

Schools

Sixteenth-century Protestant manifestos had as much to say about education as about dogma and Scotland has long been perceived as a country that values teaching and learning. The Reformation did not initiate schooling. There were already plenty of prestigious and long-established burgh grammar schools: for example, at Glasgow (1124) and Dundee (1239). Laws providing for schools and schoolmasters to be funded by landowners or 'heritors' in all rural parishes were passed in 1617, 1633, and 1696, but (like most early legislation) they initially expressed aspiration rather than announced achievement.

Parish schools gradually established themselves and their achievements can be seen in literacy levels. Medieval literacy was restricted to perhaps 10% of men and less than one-third of Lowland men were able to sign the mid-17th-century Covenants for themselves. Had they been given the chance, only 10% of women could have done so and 10% was the likely male literacy rate in the Highlands. By the mid-18th century, a majority of Lowland men and one-third of women could sign and many more could read. With rising incomes, printing became a powerful motor for raising Scottish literacy, especially in the form of cheap pamphlets. Still the Highlands lagged, despite initiatives by bodies

7. Many rural Scots were Godly, temperate people with a strong belief in education

like the Society in Scotland for Propagating Christian Knowledge (established in 1709 by royal authority and with later government cash injections). Literacy of professionals had had a part to play in a vibrant Highland culture, but this tradition was moribund by the 18th century and mass culture was more oral, spontaneous, and participative than the structured, increasingly commercialized, and printed media of the Lowlands.

Scottish schooling was at its most successful in the age of Enlightenment, but social and economic change quickly outdated it. Early 19th-century inquiries showed large numbers of children excluded from education through the necessity of earning a living to help their impoverished families. Surveys also showed that, while the majority of male adults could read, many fewer could write, and female literacy was (as always) lower still. Voluntary providers and fee-paying education filled the gap until legislation made schooling compulsory in 1872 and free in 1890. Until then, fee-paying schools complemented the parish and burgh schools (the latter funded by town councils), becoming more important with industrialization and urbanization. Robert Burns was educated at one such 'adventure' school.

By 1910–11, Scotland had a higher proportion of children in the age group 5–14 attending school than any other European country except France. Mass education changed the composition of the teaching profession to 70% female by 1911, overturning centuries of control by 'dominies' or male teachers. Voluntarism remained as important to schooling as to other areas of civic life. Sunday Schools staffed by lay volunteers provided a training that was especially important in the industrial towns and by 1895 there were 50,000 such teachers.

Education is timeless, but its sacrifice to examination and certification is Victorian. A Leaving Certificate Examination was first introduced in 1888 and reformed in 1962. Distinctively, modern Scottish pupils mostly sit 'Standard Grade' (like English 'O Levels') at age 14–15 and 'Highers' at 15–18 though many now proceed at 17–18 to 'Advanced Highers', which are similar to 'A Levels'. All are currently part of a 'Scottish Credit and Qualifications Framework' that covers secondary and further education as a whole. Set notionally at 14 in 1883 and 15 in 1918, actual minimum school leaving age was not increased until 1901 and 1947 respectively; it became 16 in 1972.

Most Scottish education is now publicly funded and state controlled. Among English-leaning independent or private schools (what the English would class minor 'public schools') are the Edinburgh Academy (1824), which is grand; Fettes College (1870), which looks grand (called by some the 'Scots Eton'); and Trinity College, Glenalmond (Perths.) founded by Gladstone not only to anglicize but also to Anglicanize (it is Episcopalian). All were boys-only until the 1970s, but all are now co-educational. A tier down is George Heriot's, a 'Merchant Company' school originally run by a guild as an orphan's home, that is like an English endowed grammar school (with similar middle-class overtones). It too is now co-educational. For girls there was the comparable James Gillespie's High School for Girls (1930–73), attended by novelist Muriel Spark (1918–2006) and the basis for the school in *The Prime of Miss Jean Brodie* (1961). Prominent Edinburgh educational edifices include the Royal High School (1829), long the jewel of the royal burgh's publicly funded schools and nearly the home of Scotland's parliament at the time of the torpedoed devolution referendum in 1979.

Just how good Scotland's schooling was has been debated for the last two centuries. It professed egalitarianism, giving gifted but poor boys, called 'lad of parts', a chance through schooling. But beneath this ideal lay both a firmly elitist version of meritocracy and a socially conservative vision of a limited, conformist mass education as a civilizing and pacifying force. Yet for a country persistently poorer than England, the commitment to comprehensive schooling under public control in pursuit of broadly egalitarian goals is remarkable. This stems from the Reformation belief in the power of education, reinvigorated by Enlightenment faith in the improvability of humanity, together creating a proffered ideal of the educated person and the enlightened society that is more distinctive and possibly more important to Scotland than its tangible attainments.

Universities

Prior to c. 1300, Scots who went to university mostly attended Oxford or Cambridge, but after that they flooded European colleges – and continued to do so even after the foundation of three Scottish universities in the 15th century. Then it was easy to go to university abroad because there was one international language of learning, Latin, which all educated men (and a handful of women) could speak, read, and write, and because, pre-Luther and Calvin, united Christendom imposed few barriers to an international 'republic of letters'. For the brave, travel was simple (modern passports date from as late as 1915). Scots students were thus found studying theology, law, and medicine at universities like Montpellier, Padua, and Paris or, from the 1570s, at the Protestant foundation of Leiden. For Catholics, there were Scots Colleges at Paris, Rome, and Salamanca.

The 'grammar' in 'grammar school' was Latin. Until the 18th century, when lecturing in English became established, Latin was a central part of post-elementary and university education and a vocational requirement for any professional man. It also created a high culture of classics that was not only recreational, but also central to the ideology of order and hierarchy in politics and society, including later-Stewart state-building, post-1688 Jacobitism, and Enlightenment politeness. Classically based humanist literature, produced by figures like George Buchanan, also gave Scots letters international cultural standing. If there was a linguistic focus for Scottish elite identity between Renaissance and Enlightenment, it was Latin rather than either Scots, English or Gaelic.

Universities were established by charters from the pope or the Holy Roman Emperor. St Andrews (c. 1412), Glasgow (1451), and King's College, Aberdeen (1495) all have papal charters and are thus real universities. Edinburgh's 'university' (1583) has none and is properly known as a 'town's college' (as their first playing field the council gave the students five acres next to the gallows located near the present Pollock Halls of Residence); nor has Marischal College, Aberdeen (1593; united with King's in 1860). Renaissance universities acquired more colleges: at St Andrews there was St Salvator's (1450), St Leonard's (1511), and St Mary's (1538).

Reformation further regenerated universities. If John Knox was the face of the Reformation, its brain was Andrew Melville, a man of clear and uncompromising principles, who used his experience of continental universities to revitalize Glasgow and St Andrews in the 1570s and 1580s. Yet universities remained glorified seminaries, teaching mainly theology and philosophy (then a broader discipline): legal and medical training only began to flourish in the 18th century, when Edinburgh quadrupled its intake, its students English (especially Protestant Dissenters barred from Oxford and Cambridge), North American, and European as well as home-grown. Scotland's universities have always been cosmopolitan places.

Not all were equally illustrious. In the 18th century, Aberdeen and St Andrews approached the lassitude of Oxford and Cambridge. Medical degrees were awarded largely on the basis of testimonials or civic credentials, and it was said of Dr Alexander Donaldson of Marischal College in 1783 that he 'neither delivers lectures nor practices, but resides chiefly upon his estate in the neighbourhood of Aberdeen'. Still, Scotland's universities produced nine out of ten British medical graduates c. 1800. Scottish graduates of the 19th century were ineligible for fellowships in the English Royal College of Physicians and hence were excluded from London hospitals, though the capital's loss was the provinces' (and empire's) gain.

While they lacked mid-19th-century dynamism, Scotland's universities were successfully reformed in the last quarter of the century. They were cheaper to attend and thus more socially inclusive than elitist Oxford or Cambridge – at least for males, as no woman was allowed to matriculate until 1892. In the 1860s, university participation rates were five times higher than in England, yet until the 1960s less than 2% of eligible young men and women (or less than 0.2% of the population) went to university. Late Victorian reforms actually reduced the chances for working-class youth, for whom opportunities were only re-opened by student maintenance grants in the 1960s. Grants brought true egalitarianism to Scottish (and British) universities: without them no amount of tinkering will make higher education socially inclusive.

With many students burdened by debt, participation rates now approach 50% in higher education as a whole as more universities and other institutions have been founded and existing ones have grown. University education is increasingly the norm and degrees are now available in a much wider range of subjects than a generation ago: for example, at former colleges of art and design like Duncan of Jordanstone (now part of Dundee University). Four more universities came during the expansion of the 1960s and early 1970s – Stirling (brand new), Dundee (an offshoot college of St Andrews since 1881), Heriot-Watt and Strathclyde (former technical colleges) – and five more after the abolition of the 'binary divide' in higher education (1992). Scotland's biggest 'university', Edinburgh, currently has 19,000 undergraduates and 7,000 postgraduates.

Scotland's universities flourished by providing professional training, but they also emphasized freedom of choice, broad study, general or 'Ordinary' rather than honours degrees (still taken by one-third of graduates), and education as a process not an event. Ancient universities have since Victorian times conferred Master of Arts (MA) honours degrees in humanities after four years of study rather than the English Bachelor (BA) after three. Scotland's universities remain world leaders and, for those careless enough not to have been educated at Eton or 'Oxbridge', they have been seminaries for aspiring statesmen like (in the 1970s) current

British PM Gordon Brown (Edinburgh) and a string of
Conservative MPs (St Andrews).

Vocations

Medieval youth went abroad because their vision was European,
education was better, and Continental universities taught
vocational subjects such as Roman or 'civil' law, which could be
applied in Scottish courts, but which were not available at home.
There was no provision for education in Scots law comparable
with the London Inns of Court until a chair was established at
Edinburgh University in 1722. Much legal and medical training
was instead obtained by work experience. Advocates (like English
barristers) had their own Faculty (association) from c. 1532 and
Writers to the Signet (like solicitors) a Society from c. 1594.
Britain's oldest medical society, the Royal College of Surgeons of
Edinburgh, was chartered in 1506 and the quite separate Royal
College of Physicians in 1681.

Put simply, surgeons (sometimes called barber-surgeons) worked
on bodies whereas physicians (who charged more) dealt with
people. Apothecaries were tradesmen who dispensed drugs.
Physicians were usually educated at Continental universities, but
until the 18th century accredited surgeons and apothecaries were
trained by apprenticeship. Apprenticeship was still an important
part of job-training for manual occupations until the 20th century,
but by the mid-19th century medical education had become more
systematic and university-based, the profession more united as the
ancient division by training was modified.

Access to vocational training was dependent on social background,
wealth, and connections. Poor parents could send girls to spinning
schools, but those who wanted a boy apprenticed to a trade or
craft like metalworking had to pay a master 'hammerman'
(smith) to take him on. Young men who made it through their
three-to-five-year training became journeymen or employees then

masters in their own right – provided they had enough money to set up for themselves. This meant that, while Scotland may have had an egalitarian ethos and an ideal of opportunity based on talent, in reality social mobility was restricted. The same is true of the white-collar professions. Pre-modern lawyers comprised mostly the younger sons of landed families and they operated a closed shop, which the unconnected newcomer could rarely enter.

Indeed, patronage and clientage permeated historic Scotland and getting a job was as much a matter of the right networking as the right abilities. Formal qualifications were not needed for most industrial or commercial careers until the 20th century, though 'serving time' as an apprentice was the norm. Universities held some written exams, but tests both in school and for jobs were mainly verbal (if used at all) and modern ideas of careers based on merit and open competition only originated c. 1900. Yet the introduction of competitive legal examinations did not alter the social composition of the legal profession (or most others): it simply created a different avenue for those who would have entered it anyway.

Enlightenment

Alongside the drawing rooms, libraries, and even taverns of 18th-century Scotland, its universities were the crucible of the Enlightenment, an explosion of ideas which had a deep and lasting influence on the thought and practices of the English-speaking world and all those touched by it. Faith in the improvability of individual and society through education, reason, and discussion led men like Adam Ferguson (1723–1816), Adam Smith (1723–90), and David Hume (1711–76) to celebrate and promote commerce by arguing that economic co-operation and exchange would promote sociability, refinement, and 'taste'. Philosophers debated everything from what 'sympathy' meant – was it simply openness to the sentiments of others or did it require an adaptation to those feelings? – to whether it was acceptable to commit suicide. Not just academics, but any educated person, could participate, men and women meeting in dining clubs, reading societies, musical concerts, and theatres to exchange ideas and to become better people simply by being together.

Enlightenment ideas are best seen in their concrete effects. Notions of civility, equity, and improvement pervaded 19th-century Scottish society, and they help to explain the lower levels of popular protest there than in England. A widely shared faith in the value of education (whatever its actual achievements) and in the improvability of civil society made Scotland's people more interested in treading a positive and peaceful path towards progress, and made them better able to cope with change than some. Both working and middle classes were much influenced by the need for reason and argument to trump violence and irrationality.

But as well as tempering the effects of change at home, the Scottish Enlightenment also altered the world. Philosophers espoused notions of toleration and religiously inspired visions of common humanity that, for example, underpinned a Court of Session judgment in 1778 deeming slavery unsustainable in Scots law. They established the idea that change was a process not an event, and they introduced the concepts, methods, and models of natural sciences into social investigation, teaching scepticism about the sources of knowledge. Public anatomical dissections and midwifery lectures, the geology of James Hutton (1726–97), and the chemistry of Joseph Black (1728–99) made applied science an international cultural commodity alongside art, literature, music, and folklore, later exemplified in fascination with subjects as diverse as electricity and the origin of species.

Literature of the 18th century helped to construct an image of Scottish identity comprising primitive virtue, traditional humanist learning, and modern politeness that lasted throughout the 19th century. The commerce that promoted interchange and understanding also sustained a consumer revolution that brought tea, coffee, sugar, tobacco, china, and cotton fabrics to mass markets. Mundane modern civilities originated in the Enlightenment. The fork, water closet, handkerchief, and night attire were all introduced to mediate, distance, or conceal the body's necessities.

Where the French Enlightenment was militantly anti-clerical, Calvinist theology was a powerful influence on Scotland's, and many of its best minds were divines (most of them university professors). Individual thinkers like Thomas Reid (1710–96) altered the way people saw both their individuality and their society. Adam Smith's *The Wealth of Nations* (1776) provided intellectual support for '*laissez-faire*', a doctrine that lay at the heart of 19th-century Western economics. With Hume and Ferguson, he also produced the tidy distinction between impersonal utilitarian and personal affective relationships now so familiar in the instrumental, individualist West.

Scottish law, medical expertise, and its university system were all successfully exported to the wider world by missionaries, migrants, and imperial bureaucrats. Scots helped to make the British Empire what it was materially and ideologically, but they also contributed to its partial unravelling during the American Revolution. Amid extensive political conformity (university appointments were based partly on patronage), one radical strand was the Covenanters' tradition of conditional loyalty to the British state: it gradually faded in Scotland, but was transported to North America and proved enduring in Northern Ireland.

Many of the ideas now taken for granted came out of the Enlightenment, but other phenomena seem more incongruous. Grave robbing and murder were used to satisfy demand for corpses to dissect at the flourish medical schools, including the infamous Burke and Hare duo. Duelling is another example. Wrongly seen as a survival of the medieval trial by combat, where

God's hand was thought to guide the righteous victor, it was in fact a Renaissance importation from the Continent that thrived in the age of Enlightenment. Until the 19th century, the duel was a way of regulating courtesy and honour in conduct between equals. While it involved physical force, it was commonly located within long-established notions of civility or politeness rather than outside and in opposition to them. Criticisms of duelling came less from outright hostility than from dissatisfaction with the level of sincerity of participants and the propriety of the forms it took. The last duel in Scotland took place at Kirkcaldy in 1826 between a banker and dissatisfied customer. The banker died.

Duelling reminds us that this was the 18th century, not the 21st. The Scottish Enlightenment did not come out of the blue, but built on the work of 17th-century European jurists like Hugo Grotius and Samuel von Pufendorf, and on the achievements of English philosophers and scientists such as Thomas Hobbes, John Locke, and Isaac Newton, though the 18th-century English Enlightenment was neither so profuse nor so profound. Scots thinkers made the modern world, but so did many other things, and influences sometimes took decades to become clear. Yesterday's household names – like William Robertson D. D., minister of Greyfriars (1761–94), principal of Edinburgh University (1762–93), and celebrity historian of Scotland and America – are now forgotten, and those famous to posterity sometimes struggled for recognition at the time. Hume's 'deism' (a sort of atheism) horrified many contemporaries and he was shunned in his own day, lamenting that his first work, *A Treatise of Human Nature* (1738), 'dropped dead-born from the press'.

Chapter 4
Society

Population

Estimating Scotland's population is guesswork until c. 1700, when there were about a million inhabitants, but some demographic guidelines can be drawn. Roman Britain was as densely settled as Stewart Britain and the standard of living was probably as good. The first demographic landmark was the 'Black Death', a plague epidemic that affected Britain 1348–50, carrying off perhaps one-third of the population. Plague then became endemic: subsequent outbreaks were less virulent and tended to be localized to towns. Scotland's last major plague was in the mid-1640s, but there were still scares as late as 1720–1. Plague was feared as much for the disruption of social and economic life as for the threat of death. With quarantines in place, corpses were carted to mass graves without the usual observances that made their passing bearable for friends and family.

At the time of the Black Death, Europe also entered a mini-Ice Age. With fewer workers and an adverse climate, higher-altitude settlements were abandoned. Bad weather, low productivity, and poor communications meant that food shortages long remained a threat. The last serious national famine was in the late 1690s when perhaps one in eight of the population died of hunger or disease. Lowland agricultural productivity doubled or trebled in the

18th century, but bad harvests could still cause hunger and death in the 1740s and even 1810s. Most deaths during the 'Great Highland Famine' of the 1840s and 1850s were attributable to disease associated with chronic poverty and deprivation rather than to hunger alone (caused primarily by potato blight).

Expectation of life at birth was in the 30s for centuries, but if people survived infancy and childhood they could live into their 60s or 70s. In 1700, one-twelfth of the population was over 60, and during the 18th century adult male life expectancy rose by one-third. Higher fertility and lower mortality meant that the population trebled from 1.5 to 4.5 million between 1789 and 1911, a modest rate of growth that disguises the massive redistributions of people that came out of agrarian change and urbanization. As late as 1789, just under half of Scotland's people lived north of an imaginary 'Highland Line' drawn between Stonehaven (Kincardines.) in the east and Helensburgh (Dumbartons.) in the west. By 1911, this had fallen to just one-sixth. One Scot in eight lived in a large town in 1790, one in three by 1831, and three out of five in 1911, by which date Scotland was the most urbanized country in Europe after England. In the 1890s, one-quarter of the adult population of Glasgow had been born in the Highlands and another quarter in Ireland.

Mortality from disease remained high, but it was falling. Smallpox was conquered by the early 19th century, but typhus and cholera continued to decimate urban populations until mid-century and influenza until 1918. Infant mortality rates were lower in Scotland than England, but still alarmingly high, and they did not fall as they did in England from the 1890s. Of those born around 1871, one-quarter would not live to the age of five.

Scotland's 19th-century fertility regime was also distinctive. Women married exceptionally late by European standards (usually in their late 20s – one-fifth did not marry at all) but, once married, fertility was high. Late marriage was the most effective check on fertility. It could also be limited by prolonged breastfeeding, sexual abstinence, or basic contraceptive techniques such as withdrawal. Modern 'birth control', using mechanical methods to choose how many children to have and when, was an early 20th-century development. Its introduction was led mainly by men, until the Pill gave women greater control in the 1960s.

Family size fell dramatically. Two-fifths of marriages made in the 1870s produced more than six children compared with less than 2% for 1920s marriages. Scotland's illegitimacy was generally low, but in pockets it was amongst the highest in Europe: in the rural north-east, four-fifths of women marrying in the late 19th century had their first child before, or within three months of, marriage. Throughout the 19th century, Scotland was a young society, one-third of its people aged 14 years or younger.

Modern Scotland has roughly five million inhabitants and its demography is comparable with much of Western Europe and North America, notably the 'greying' of the population. Birth rates are low and, despite longer life expectancy, the indigenous population is falling. The social structures that once contained demographic activity have changed enormously in the last generation. Half of all women marrying under age 30 had cohabited prior to marriage in the late 1980s, compared with just 3% in the 1960s. The year 1997 was the first when more than half of Dundee births were to single mothers or to cohabiting but unmarried partners, and across Scotland 25% of children now live in one-parent families. At 1987 rates, one-third of marriages of the late 1970s will end in divorce, compared with just 7% of marriages contracted in the early 1950s. Thanks partly to conservative education policies, seemingly based on the premise that not teaching sexual health will prevent young people having sex, rates of teenage pregnancy and sexually transmitted disease are among the highest in Europe.

8. An aerial view of St Andrews, showing the cathedral, castle, and the east end of the medieval three-street plan. Since the Middle Ages, Scottish towns were centres of church, government, trade, and learning

Living standards

Scotland was not a wealthy country for much of its history and it dealt with its poor in different ways from England. Since Elizabethan times, English poor relief was nationally organized, but locally administered and financed, combining core provision by rating of richer inhabitants with informal giving. Scotland had early legislation like England's, but it was never effectively enforced and the balance of provision was exactly reversed. Taxation for this (or any other) purpose remained deeply unpopular. Instead, a mixed economy of welfare sustained the needy with the focus on informal giving. Towns had rates, but in rural parishes the Church, landowners, and neighbours provided most doles until the Kirk took over the administration of formal relief in the 17th century. The system often struggled to cope and became more strained as population was redistributed to towns and as the Kirk fragmented.

The 1845 poor law for Scotland, coming on the heels of economic collapse 1841–3 (in Paisley 67 of 112 manufacturers went bankrupt and one-quarter of the population was on poor relief) and the Disruption (1843), was designed to facilitate levying rates, though these remained almost unknown in the Highlands. Yet the extent of local autonomy in policy-making remained much greater than in England and the reality of poor relief was quite different. Scottish local government had long had a more directive attitude towards public health and, unlike its English equivalent of 1834, the 1845 poor law required personal medical care for paupers, a provision whose spirit survives in the present Scottish parliament's healthcare policy for the elderly.

Nearly all Victorian orphans were cared for in foster homes; the Scots did not want the coming generation exposed to the bad example of the poorhouse. Fostering was deemed to be better psychologically and financially for children and foster parents, and it was cheaper for the parish than institutionalization (local accountability often meant curtailing expenditure). Indeed, a signal difference was the lack of formal institutions for the poor, with a preference for domestic or 'outdoor' relief rather than the grim, degrading English workhouses. In 1906, 14% of Scotland's pauper population received institutionalized or 'indoor' relief, compared with 32% in England.

Historically, most poor people were women because they usually outlived men and had less chance to save by exclusion from higher-paying employments, being paid less for the same job, having interrupted working lives because of care responsibilities, and (until Victorian times) suffering legal restrictions on owning savings in their own right. Introduced in 1909 for the over-70s, British old-age pensions were designed partly to cope with these issues, but they were set below subsistence to encourage saving, work, or dependence on family. The means-tested benefits also carried a social stigma.

Despite growing British prosperity after c. 1750 and the reorganization of poor relief after 1845, Scotland's standard of living lagged behind England's. In 1867, 70% of 'productive persons' earned less than £30 per annum, while the top 10% gobbled up half the national income. Wealth polarization was especially pronounced in towns and is shown in housing. The urban poor moved into the central homes the middle class vacated on their way to Georgian 'New Towns' and Victorian suburbs, and also the new, but often badly built, 'tenements' (apartment buildings) that housed the industrial labour force of mushrooming towns like Paisley. In 1911, over half the Scottish population lived in one- or two-roomed homes, and in Glasgow and Dundee the figure was over 60%. Overcrowding was the result, with nearly 56% of Glaswegians living more than two to a room.

Diet depended for centuries on population pressure and the limitations of agriculture. Middens (rubbish dumps) show that Scots binged on beef during Iron Age and Dark Age rituals, and the English on pork, suggesting these meats were not staples. Flesh-eating may have returned in the late Middle Ages, but most Scots had a fish- and vegetarian-leaning diet c. 1550–1750 because meat was too expensive. Immortalized by English artist William Hogarth in *The Gate of Calais* (1749), (roast) beef was a standard dietary item and a cultural icon of England. Best known from its association with Burns Suppers, haggis (chopped mutton offal, oatmeal, and onion in a stomach lining) is less authentic an historic 'signature' dish than the humble (and healthy) herring or, for carnivores, lamb shank or sheep's head. The latter featured in

Mrs Beeton's Victorian *Book of Household Management*, but is currently served nowhere, though the 'Sheep Heid Inn', one of Scotland's oldest pubs at Duddingston, Edinburgh, used to until banned in the early 1980s. Diet improved as agricultural productivity rose, and industrial and commercial success allowed food to be imported, but rickets was still a common condition for working-class urban children until the 20th century.

Modern Scotland has a reputation for alcohol abuse and general ill-health encapsulated in soberingly low adult (male) life expectancy and exemplified by the deep-fried Mars Bar. Yet many of the problems are related not to race, but to divisions of social class and economic opportunity that have equivalents across Britain and Europe. The post-1945 welfare state helped greatly to improve nutrition and life expectancy, while the Clean Air Act of 1956 was the first major modern environmental measure. Health-awareness has improved dramatically in the last generation as living standards too approach European averages, with appreciably less smoking, better diet, and more exercise. Having the 2014 Commonwealth Games in Glasgow can only help.

Most Scots nowadays are concerned with selecting what to eat rather than finding enough. Until the 1980s, eating out in restaurants was unusual and the food mostly boring and poorly prepared – prawn cocktail the height of sophistication. Now smart country-house hotels abound and it is easy to eat out well (if far from cheaply). Scottish chefs like Nick Nairn and Hamish Wishart are world class – as is Gordon Ramsay in London. Oddly for a nation whose elites spent centuries buying eagerly from Bordeaux, Oporto, and the Rhineland, wine consumption was low until the late 20th century. Alcohol has never been cheaper in real terms and will be the next target of the health lobby now that the message about tobacco has been enforced. Pioneered by California (1994) and Ireland (2004), Scotland introduced a ban on smoking in public places in 2006.

Whisky was a working-class drink from the 17th century and a headache for moral reformers, just as gin was in 18th-century England. Like most symbols of modern Scotland, whisky's current cachet is a marketing triumph. Historically, the civilized spirit was brandy, smuggled if possible to avoid duty, and the preferred drink was wine or port. Until the 18th century, towns set wine prices every year just as they did the price of grain. Beer or ale (made with malted barley rather than hops) was as much a foodstuff as a recreational beverage – and a lot less risky than drinking water for townspeople until 19th-century improvements in sanitation reduced deadly diseases like cholera and typhoid.

Scots were highly mobile people for centuries, but they were not tourist travellers. When Scot James Boswell and his Scottophobic English chum Samuel Johnson toured and wrote about the western Highlands and Islands in 1773, they were not the first 'tourists'. Early Scottish travel writer Martin Martin did it in the 1690s, clergyman Rev. John Walker in the 1760s, and the Welsh naturalist and antiquary Thomas Pennant in 1769 and 1772. But Johnson's complaints about the food, including hair in the butter, echo through the centuries. Commercial inns existed from the 17th century, mostly for cattle drovers, and there were lodging houses in towns, but until the 19th century there was a strong tradition of rural hospitality and most travellers who wanted food and lodging simply called at any promising farmhouse: the equivalent of the modern B&B. Landed gentry used family or social connections to stay with each other on a knock-for-knock basis.

A 'holy day' was literally a day off and more prolonged travel for leisure was unusual before the 20th century, except for the handful of nobles who went on the Grand Tour of Europe. Scots worked a 6-day, 55-hour week until 1919, and paid leave was unknown until 1938; for domestic servants, still one-eighth of the employed population in 1911, work hours could be limitless. Two-week holidays became more common in the 1930s, when rail travel expanded and car ownership first mushroomed, but there was still extensive Saturday working into the 1950s.

Like most post-war Britons, Scots holidayed at domestic seaside resorts such as Largs, Rothesay, or North Berwick. For the adventurous middle class there was the ski centre at Aviemore, hideously refurbished and extended in the 1960s (recently made over again), and for the fun-loving working class, holiday camps like Butlins at Ayr. Air travel was the preserve of the rich, holidaying abroad was unusual, and mass tourism did not begin in earnest until the 1960s. Modern Scots are avid sun-seekers, carbon-neutral or otherwise, and, for the time being, it is possible to fly directly (and cheaply) from Scottish airports to destinations around the world.

Aristocrats and people

The most common social and cultural label applied by the English to Scotland is 'Celtic fringe', a classification that usually also includes Wales, Ireland, Brittany, and Galicia in Spain. However, both Celtic identity and origins are vague. The usual picture is of population migration from central Europe to Britain and Ireland some time in the 1st millennium BC, the supposed migrants bringing language, culture, and material objects. Cultural change certainly happened, but was it the result of immigration (peaceful or otherwise) or of more gradual adaptation of existing ideas and technologies? DNA analysis shows that most modern Britons descended from the post-glacial colonizers of 10,000 years ago, and only the genetic profile of northern Scotland is distinctive for its Scandinavian admixture.

Of course, DNA modelling is based on modern populations and its apparent accuracy does not necessarily make it appropriate to the past. Chromosomes do not tell us about migrations within zones that shared a gene pool, notably the probable settlement of the Isle of Man and Argyll in the 5th century AD by Gaels from Ireland,

and nor do genes predict cultural identity. Modern 'Celts' define themselves largely on the basis of a language distinct from the Germanic tongues that include English, but there is no evidence that the Celts were defined by their language prior to the Renaissance. The idea that they settled Britain and Ireland originated with the 16th-century writer George Buchanan, who identified them with a language he called 'Gallic', later termed 'Celtic' by the Welsh scholar Edward Lhuyd in his *Archaeologia Britannica* (1707). The word 'Celt' was not current between antiquity and Buchanan: nobody in the Dark or Middle Ages thought they were Celts, and the term is a modern taxonomic convenience. The terms 'Gael' and 'Pict' were used by contemporaries much as modern observers do, but 'Celt' was mined by antiquarians to create a pseudo-Linnaean classificatory grouping for the purpose of ordering the past.

The other historic identifier of the Celts is their art, a distinctive material culture c. 500 BC to c. AD 900 characterized by swords, broaches, mirrors, and other works found across Europe. 'Celtic art', with its dynamic abstract and zoomorphic patterns, is sometimes called 'La Tène' style from its 'type site' in modern Switzerland, where the first examples were discovered. This too was a later description, given in the 19th century to the artefacts produced by pre-Roman inhabitants of Britain and Ireland, who were thought to be Celts. This style is also found among non-Celtic speakers and was never adopted by the Celtic-speaking peoples of Spain. Both language and art may have emerged independently in different parts of Europe, influencing and being influenced by pre-Celtic forms.

Peaceful settlement almost certainly did *not* take place in later Orkney. Genetic profiling has shown that most males on the island have a Norse DNA signature and the only non-Norse can be traced to those who arrived in Orkney after the island was annexed by Scotland in 1469 (Christian I of Denmark mortgaged the Northern Isles to James II's son when he married his daughter in

1468). The inference is that Pictish males, who were the indigenous people in the 9th century, were ejected, exterminated, or prevented from breeding by being reduced to servitude, for slavery was an integral part of Dark Age and early medieval society. Across northern Scotland, distinctively Pictish culture also seems to have disappeared in the 10th century, though not for the same reasons as in Orkney because the Pictish people remained.

The best that can be said about society before the Middle Ages is that it was hierarchical, for the Norse threat had created a new focus on sustaining a military class answerable to the king. It was also strongly based on customary law and on family and kinship networks. 'Celtic' influence was one of many. After 1100, generalizations are easier. The Anglo-Normans introduced feudalism, at whose core was a bond between an assigner of land and its assignee that entailed clearly specified rights and obligations. Gaelic society was less socially rigid, based on a kindred or 'clan', where moral obligations were intensely strong, but rights hardly ever specified.

Yet there were important similarities between clan or client society and the feudal system, which were used by the crown to equate local with central and royal with lordly interests. The bonds that made both were personal rather than impersonal and vertical rather than horizontal, going between master and man, lord and vassal (dependant), patron and client, father and family. During the 12th century, the basic division in society ceased being freeman/slave and became lord/peasant, but the existence into the early 17th century of a 'common army' alongside knight service shows that the Scottish peasantry was freer than most in Europe and that the feudal revolution there was mediated by existing social and legal assumptions.

Both social organizations depended less on wealth, though that could be accumulated in the form of people, land, or livestock, than on the circulation of gifts. Control of industrial products like weapons and jewellery was one way lords expressed and enhanced their power, as was law-giving, benevolence to the poor, and patronage of cultural activities such as poetry and medicine. Status in the medieval Gaelic world (and probably in the Dark Ages too) was measured by the number of alliances and the number and standing of a man's followers. But above all, it was based on gifts, hospitality, and the frequent assigning and receiving of livestock and land. These 'goods' were acquired and given through fighting, feasting, and patronage: things that meant as much for their symbolism as for their material value. In feudal terms, the king completed a gift of land, but left the recipient with an incomplete or open-ended commitment of service.

One way in which feudalism did change Scottish society more than English was in the confirmation of devolved or delegated noble power over justice and taxation, a tendency firmly resisted by English kings. Scottish nobles had probably always had considerable independent power over their people, but after c. 1100 they institutionalized an arms-length relationship with the crown by securing extensive judicial rights and associated financial privileges. This independence was eroded from the time of James VI, but not removed until 1748. Even then, the aristocracy retained some of their courts (with much limited powers) and were compensated for the loss of what were, after all, rights of property.

This was a face-to-face society where a person's reputation, social and moral as well as economic, was his or her 'credit'. Having a lord was not a mark of failure, because lords were supposed to defend and promote their underlings: the stronger the lord, the better-off the vassal, and vice versa. The ability of landowners to act independently was closely circumscribed by the obligations of lordship: sometimes lords could be the instruments of their tenants rather than vice versa.

Until Adam Smith taught them to distinguish economic utility from personal feelings, Scots (and English) treated economics very personally – almost morally. Only from the mid-18th century did impersonal market forces play a growing role in mediating between people. This produced the 'class' society that the German thinker Karl Marx made famous in *Capital* (1867). A shared group consciousness derived from experience of working life (like coal-mining or factory labour), expressing itself in social, cultural, and political ways as diverse as trade unions, the press, education, and the search for representation.

In 19th- and 20th-century class society, the middle and working classes pursued interests that were often separate and sometimes conflicting, exemplified in the formation of the Labour Party to represent manual labour. Prior to this, society was dominated by landowning nobilities, who were as numerous in Scotland as in England – which had five times as many inhabitants. It is hard to underestimate the importance of the aristocracy prior to the 20th century: selfishness, greed, and parsimony over public services there surely was, but from a sense of duty as well as self-interest, nobles kept society and government running when kingship was weak; some landmark events were made by people of clear principle and radical intent, notably the Reformation and the Scottish Revolution; and the aristocracy was central to the agricultural and industrial revolutions. Of course, the rich and powerful leave the biggest footprint of their individuality. The flamboyant James Graham, Marquis of Montrose, may have fought (brilliantly) on the wrong (Royalist) side and come to a sticky end in 1650, but he had a lot more style than his Covenanting opponents.

Being colourful may excuse much, but there was a serious social cost to noble dominance of society, especially in the rural world. Most of those who worked the land did not own it. 'Feuing', notably of church land before and after the Reformation, helped create a class of lesser owner-occupiers, or 'lairds' (lords), who were close economically to English yeomen freeholders (though far less numerous) and socially to the gentry, yet there were just

7,500 landowners in Scotland c. 1830, and in the 1870s 1,500 of them owned 90% of the land. Leases were often short and tenants could easily be removed from their land for not paying their rent.

Beneath the tenants was a numerous but shadowy rural proletariat of sub-tenants, or 'cottars' (cottagers), who made up one-third of the medieval and early-modern population and who were even less secure. One of the things that made the Scots so adaptable and eager to assimilate abroad (and thus often ethnically invisible among white populations) was that they were so used to uncertainty, change, and mobility at home. There was no equivalent of the most famous English rising, the 1381 Peasants' Revolt, because personal servitude had disappeared from Scotland by the mid-14th century; heavy or regular taxation was disliked by all social classes and was thus avoided; and because the economic and social hold of Scots lords over the peasantry was much stronger than in England.

Scotland's fluid and malleable rural society explains the ease with which monumental changes took place in the 18th and 19th centuries. By the 1820s, Lowland society had become polarized between landowners, tenants, and landless labourers, most sub-tenants and many smaller tenants having been swept from the land. In the Lothians, the labourers were mostly married men paid largely in kind. Elsewhere in Scotland (such as the north-east), both smallholders and single servants (both living-in and out-housed in 'bothies' or dormitories) provided the labour that in England came from workers hired by the day. Additional labour needs were met by women, children, and (for the arable Lowlands) seasonal migrant workers from the Highlands.

Structured dependency accounts for the absence of anything like the southern English 'Captain Swing' riots of 1830. Displaced rural Scots of the 19th century had employment alternatives in the towns or overseas, while in the countryside the power of landowners remained great. For one working-class autobiographer, a Borders shoemaker, the lord was 'protected by his influence and power of patronage, mail proof against all the tiger-claws of justice: indeed, he is the hereditary maker of what is called country justice'. Religion too provided justifications for quiescence as well as assertiveness.

That is not to say there was no opposition to social and economic change. Less in thrall to landowners, townspeople were more demonstrative, if far fewer in number prior to the industrial revolution. For example, in 1615, the Queen's chamberlain and his officers were attacked and beaten in Burntisland by a crowd of women of the 'bangster [unruly] Amazon kind' intent on preventing them enforcing a court order. Food riots convulsed some 18th-century towns, and anything that looked like unavoidable taxation was liable to meet stiff resistance. There were true radicals during the Napoleonic period and a serious 'insurrection' in 1820.

There were more subtle ways of making a social and political point. Unpopular landlords or employers could be undermined by moving elsewhere (sometimes *en masse*), gossip, satire, or covert violence. Some religious innovation was vigorously challenged and religious divisions could express class differences. One Free Church congregation worshipped on a floating barge moored on Loch Sunart when the laird banned worship on his land. And there were the courts and political lobbying; 19th-century trades unions, like earlier craft and journeymen associations, tended to act within the law, on principles of equity and morality, to better their experience as employees rather than wholly to change a society in which they felt they had a stake. The late 19th-century Free Church worked with Highland crofters (small farmers) to secure legal changes in tenure. Even the weak had weapons.

Yet noble power was everywhere and the landscape too bears their mark. Nucleated villages existed from the 12th century in the south-east, but elsewhere farm settlements were dispersed until the 18th-century agricultural revolution, the landscape more reminiscent of Scandinavia than of England. Remodelling the landscape was legally simple for landowners. Enclosure acts, that comprised a substantial proportion of English local legislation, were unnecessary in Scotland because acts of the late 17th century consolidated landlords' rights to do more or less what they liked with their land. The results are visible in 130 distinctive planned villages built c. 1780–1850. They include Colinsburgh (Fife), Edzell (Angus), and New Pitsligo (Aberdeens.) and full-scale towns like Inveraray (Argylls.) – razed in the 1760s and 1770s and wholly rebuilt thereafter. All are testaments to the vision of landowners for regularity in the new, improved landscape and to their wealth and power in imposing it. The pleasing uniformity of 18th-century 'New Town' developments also stemmed from owners' ability to specify elevations when feuing land to builders (Chapter 7).

Planned villages solved the problem of what to do with families cleared from the land who were still required to provide labour in agriculture, their people making ends meet by crafts like weaving. The purely industrial equivalent was New Lanark, founded in 1785 as a cotton mill and model community by reformer Robert Owen. He believed wholeheartedly in education, not only for children, but also for adults at his tellingly named 'Institute for the Formation of Character' (1816). Landlord policy even touched sex and marriage. Comparison between the adjacent parishes of Grange and Rothiemay (Banffs.) on the one hand, and the island of Tiree in the Inner Hebrides on the other, reveals how landlord policies profoundly influenced demographic practices and population levels in agrarian Scotland in the late 18th and early 19th centuries. Amalgamation of farms and enclosure of common land in Banffshire forced up the age of marriage by making it more difficult for couples to establish their own households, in turn leading to a decline in the birth rate and a stagnant population; illegitimacy rates approached 30% in 1871.

On Tiree, by contrast, early marriage and a relatively low rate of celibacy was maintained by the policy of the dukes of Argyll to create crofts and subdivide tenancies, contributing ultimately to overpopulation and poverty.

Until the 19th century, governments were effectively comprised of aristocrats and those they controlled. Kings supported their ruling elites because it was impossible to govern without successful nobility. They bailed out the failures and they happily sold honours to the aspiring and successful. In 1611, James VI/I invented baronetcies – hereditary, but not true peerages – to fund an army in Ulster and extended the scheme to Scotland in 1625, where it was used to establish the colony of Nova Scotia. Much later, PM Lloyd George put sales on a business footing, but the Honours Act (1925) did not end abuses, and it remains to be seen if the Political Parties Act (2000) will succeed.

For millennia, most people lived on the land and it was *the* source of food, energy, raw materials, social status, and political influence. Land still has cachet, reinforced by extreme polarization of ownership: 88% of Scotland's rural land is in private ownership and two-thirds is owned by 1,250 people (one-quarter is in the hands of just 66 families). It is fortunate that Scots law has for centuries allowed near universal access to land for walkers and others prepared to use it responsibly.

However, the economic power of the land has gone. Death duties and changing sources of wealth combined with intensifying urbanization and democratization to rob the 20th-century aristocracy of resources and influence. George V detached the monarchy from the aristocracy with the new honours system introduced in 1917 to reward public service and the voluntary sector. Successful modern nobles like the Duke of Argyll (whose family had wealth, social clout, and enormous political influence for centuries) and the Earl of Moray have made the transition by modernizing estate management and diversifying into housing and tourism. Modern Scotland has the super-rich, but they are businesspeople and the society is fundamentally bourgeois.

Highlands

Some non-Scots think that the Highlands *are* Scotland, but in reality they are only a part, which in important ways was and is very different from the Lowlands. The Highlands were nevertheless crucial in making historic Scotland and in creating some of the tensions which underlay Scottish identity.

For reasons of geography alone, the Highlands and Islands have always been apart. The Romans got as far as the Moray Firth and Edward I too, but they and others in between retreated rather than face the Highlands proper, the Romans behind the Antonine Wall (between rivers Forth and Clyde) then Hadrian's Wall (Tyne to Solway). Their other frontier was the sea, for Romans did not dominate either the North Sea or the Irish Sea and thus allowed the continued ebb and flow of influence and counter-influence between Scotland, north-west Europe, Scandinavia, and Ireland. Communications remained difficult until improvements in roads and bridges were made for military purposes after Culloden. Yet as late as the 1960s, it could take 4 hours *by car* to journey the 50 miles between Fort William and the end of the Ardnamurchan peninsula (the furthest westerly point of mainland Britain).

Geographical differences went with a long history of political and social separation. One reason for the successful formation of the medieval Scottish kingdom was that monarchs accepted the different traditions of its component parts, Gaels as much as Britons. But political relations with the crown (and Lowlanders) changed during the early 14th century as the well-integrated magnates of central-Highland chiefdoms were replaced by lesser chiefs whose status was defined by warfare, destabilizing order and government. Highland society had long been different from

Lowland, but that difference crystallized from the 14th century as rulers turned against one part of their heritage, those they came to see as the 'wyld wikked hielandmen'.

Highland society was superficially simpler than Lowland, because its economy comprised largely farming and fishing and there were hardly any towns. In terms of relationships and attitudes, it was far more complex. Three main segments were distinguished by their relationship to land and to each other. First were the owners, the chiefs of the Middle Ages, who left estate management to middlemen (usually cadets of the main family) called 'tacksmen', who in turn rented to sub-tenants and then to crofters and cottars. A tack was like a lease, though Scottish leases were merely accounted a right of occupancy, not of property as in England.

Highland society underwent change as the landlords' and/or the tacksmen's priorities shifted during the 18th century. Many effectively repudiated centuries of being not so much landlords, as chiefs in charge of clans built on the bonds created by kinship, feuding, feasting, and gifting. The obligations of stewardship and care that owners and/or tacksmen repudiated between c. 1700 and 1900 seem vague, but they were both intensely felt and greatly valued by the peasantry. The central understanding was called *duthchas* (heritable proprietorship), which meant that the lord held his land in trust for those under him, entailing strong but unwritten obligations. As in the Lowlands, those with written title had rights, those without had none except what the lord would grant for his own reasons. Land tenure made society highly fluid. Some people really did farm the same land for generations, but tenant turnover in the Highlands was for centuries every bit as extensive as in the Lowlands. Most farmers held at will (or whim) and there was little continuity at a township or 'toun' level, even in the 17th century.

Landowners generally accommodated peasant interests while maintaining the large 'client base' that mattered to them. Initially they responded to 18th-century population growth, economic shifts, and their own changing priorities by trying to redistribute labour supply, as their power enabled them to do. However, over time they resorted to wholesale evictions or to plantations in overcrowded and economically marginal fishing villages or in industrial enterprises that lacked staying power (like harvesting kelp from the sea to make fertilizer). Later they tried emigration schemes.

Depopulation is not the whole story. Benign landlord policy and ample employment in fishing allowed the population of Lewis to grow from 17,000 to 29,000 1841–1901. Nevertheless, Highland Scotland as a whole was progressively stripped of people and migration to the Lowlands and overseas in the 18th and 19th centuries produced a lasting legacy of grievance that has no real counterpart in the Lowlands, adding to the profound historical differences between the regions. The 19th-century Highlands experienced social upheavals which, in their depth and breadth, were without parallel anywhere in Europe.

In the present day, 90% of Scotland's people live in the Lowlands, most of them in towns and cities of the central belt. Scotland has one-third of Britain's land area, one-tenth of its population, and the density of people in the Highlands is just 23 per square mile (8,550 in Glasgow). Tracts of the north-west remain empty of any habitation or indeed large animals except deer. Yet in 1755, half Scotland's population lived in the north and west, where there were plainly resources to maintain a substantial population as well as to feast on, fight over, and gift away. Cattle droving from the Highlands and Islands to feed Lowlanders (and later even English towns) was big business from the 17th century.

The extent of historic depopulation is truly staggering. Skye supported 23,000 people in 1841, 10,000 a century later. More extreme is Tiree, present population 700 outside the surfing season, which had more than 5,000 souls in 1831.

The Highlands and Scottish identity

Conventional understandings of Scottish migration focus on dispossessed Highlanders, but that is only part of the story (see Chapter 6). Highland images also play a disproportionate part in modern conceptions of Scotland's past. Once more, the reality is more complex. In fact, the association of the material aspects of Highland life – heather and thistles, bagpipes and tartan – with the symbols of being Scottish was created in London during the 18th-century romantic revival, cemented in the 1810s and 1820s by a brilliant public relations exercise by the great Tory and monarchist, the novelist Sir Walter Scott (1771–1832), and institutionalized by Queen Victoria (1837–1901).

Scott's novels had already sown the seeds when, recognizing the new monarch George IV (1820–30) needed a make-over, he stage-managed his visit to Edinburgh in 1822 (the first since Charles II's coronation in 1651). Scott's 1822 production was at one level gloriously daft, the overweight king, poured into pseudo-Highland dress, toasting the 'clans and chieftains of Scotland', whom his ancestors had tried to emasculate. At another, it was profoundly shrewd, publicizing a successful new image for Scotland that was parallel with the political subordination of the Union, but which anchored a unified national identify to the Hanoverians.

Scott helped popularize the romantic image of the Scot-as-Highlander. One of his props was tartan and another was the kilt, a skirt invented by an Englishman in the 1720s: Highlanders traditionally wore bolts of cloth called 'plaids' that could fall off the hips or be gathered like trousers. Reinvented by clever marketing of a fabricated association with names or clans – even Lowland ones – tartan gained its importance as a national symbol by being a component of Scotto-British imperialism.

As a type of cultural patriotism, this manufactured Jacobitism or Gaelicism was again just a part of being British. Begun in 1842, Queen Victoria's sincere love affair with the Highlands gave the image durability and 'Balmoralized' the royal family ever since. She bought the Aberdeenshire estate of Balmoral in 1848 and it has been the Windsors' holiday home ever since. Seeking reconciliation rather than failing to appreciate the irony, she and her husband, Prince Albert, were happy to wear Stewart tartans as well as their own inventions.

Scott has more to answer for as he turned the unacceptable face of the Highlands into something admirable. Robert MacGregor (later Campbell) or Rob Roy (1671–1734) was a (plausible and likeable) cattle thief, fraudster, extortionist, and turncoat, ramped into a Scottish version of Robin Hood by self-publicity and a fanciful biographer before becoming a national cultural icon under Scott's pen in 1818: a sort of kitsch crook. Scott manufactured an acceptable Scottishness to protect the Hanoverian dynasty and the imperial experiment, appreciating the hybrid nature of Scottish society and inviting his post-Jacobite, post-Enlightenment readers to embrace diversity in a unified identity that acknowledged what political stability and economic change had done for them.

Scott's ideological creation was a compromise that never quite came to terms with the antagonism shown by Lowlanders to the Highlands since the Renaissance. At the time many Lowlanders were appalled by the apparent glorification of what they saw as barbarism and backwardness. Their attitudes were confirmed and extended when Irish immigration began in earnest from the 1820s. Later presented as progressive, assiduous, mannerly, and orderly (when not being parodied), Victorian Scots had a far better press than the Irish, in turn written up as ungrateful, lazy, vicious, and semi-barbaric. Yet there was always the uncomfortable sense that there was more than a touch of the Irish about Highlanders. In their ambivalence towards Highlanders in the 18th century, and to Highlanders and Irish in the 19th, Lowland Scots displayed a sense of racial identity that the English lacked. Lowlanders saw the pursuit of Liberalism, free trade, and economic improvement having not an ethnic basis in a shared national history, but as immutable racial characteristics.

When, stimulated by ethnological endeavours across Europe, some 19th-century Scots intellectuals looked for a racial basis for their nation, asking 'Who are the Scots?', they found no common descent. Instead there was only a confusion of identities and, crucially, a downgraded component (Scottish Gaeldom) that was distinctive, but at odds with British Anglo-Saxondom (whose Scottish dimension included a claim for the Pictish not Gaelic origins of the nation). The fact that Scotland never had a single (or even a simple) ethnic background meant that efforts to create nationalism on the continental model were doomed. Lowlanders' partly shared identity with the English meant that most Scots tended enthusiastically to endorse Union, involvement in empire, and the more calm, rational, and decent monarchical alternative to the dangerous nationalisms of post-1848 Europe. Lowlanders in particular saw Scotland's Gaelic heritage as at worst an embarrassment and at best a side-show. One of the many contradictions in past and present Scottish nationalism is this confused sense of ethnic identity (Who are the Scots like?).

Feared, misunderstood, denigrated, or sentimentalized, Scottish Highlanders retained distinctive social and cultural characteristics as well as showing elements of 'Scottishness' and 'Britishness'. Elites tried to bridge the gap with the Lowlands by placing the Highlands in a mutually supportive relationship with other parts of Britain, emphasizing how it provided troops and foodstuffs for empire. Yet Highland society itself remained divided by wealth, education, language, and outlook during the 19th century. Scott's contemporary James Hogg (1770–1835) and later Dr Charles

Mackay (1814–89) produced anthologies of song that implied a unified culture, but again ignored both past and present social and cultural stratification.

If some Highlanders sought integration, others reacted by seeking to bolster their own separate identity through, for example, the foundation of the Free Presbyterian Church in 1893. A fading Gaelic language was another focus (see Chapter 7). Scottish history is made up of countervailing influences between the native and the external, between independence and subordination, but it is also shaped by tensions within Scotland itself of which the most profound historically was Highland-Lowland.

The modern Highlands

More important than language, ethnicity, or religion to Highlanders' identity was their emotional and material relationship to family, community, and land. From the Dark Ages to the 20th century, Highland mentalities have been pervaded by linked senses of kin and place mediated through access to land.

The most obvious manifestation was in robust traditions of opposition to what Highlanders saw as betrayal by their erstwhile chiefs. Forcible ejections produced protests in the early and mid-19th century, but later campaigns were more constructive, using the vague but important idea of *duthchas* and the resources of centuries-old memories to restore expropriated land to the descendants of those who had once cultivated it. Beginning in the 1880s, 'Land Raids' continued into the 1920s and are commemorated both in the folk song and poetry of the time and in the elegiac sculptures of modern Fife artist Will Maclean (1941–) in the now barren landscapes of the Western Isles.

Political tension between the long ingrained concepts of dual ownership and owner-occupation existed in the Highlands between 1886 and the 1920s. Liberals sought to reduce the landowners' influence by granting security of tenure to the crofters; the Conservatives wished to release the landowner from his unremunerative croft land and grant the crofter owner-occupation. Reforms proceeded. The 1883 Napier Commission helped settle disputes over rent and tenure, while the 1886 Crofters' Holdings Act reduced the landowners' influence over the crofters. An Act of 1897 could have revolutionized the Highlands, but the situation required a change of attitude towards both agriculture and husbandry that was shunned by the crofters. The farming community itself was divided, not only between owners and occupiers of land, but also between crofters, who held a small plot of land, and cottars, who were labourers or tolerated squatters. Crofters wanted lower rents, security of tenure (not necessarily ownership), and larger, more viable crofts; cottars just wanted crofts; all wanted recently fenced-off grazing restored. For the Victorian and Edwardian crofter, land was symbolic of security and status.

Land remains important, but modern Highland identity focuses more on its status as an underdeveloped region and on the political pursuit of economic and social advantage from government or EU. This tendency began in the early 19th century, when the first major public works programme in British history was tried out on the Highlands as the Treasury spent heavily on roads and bridges to improve infrastructure and create jobs. It was consolidated in 1965 with the establishment of the Highlands and Island Development Board. Current success is shown by rising population, especially on Skye, whereas that of Scotland as a whole is falling.

Obstacles to regeneration remain. Some people have a romantic vision of the Highlands, but it is a difficult environment and its people had hard lives. Highland emigration in the 20th century was mainly of young people seeking to escape not 'clearances' (the emotive description of forcible population redistribution), but the self-exploitation of the family farm. The island of St Kilda was completely evacuated in 1930 at the request of its inhabitants.

Finding work now can be difficult and housing even harder. Unlike Norway or the Netherlands, no legislation restricts non-local or non-national ownership of homes and land in Scotland. PM Margaret Thatcher sold off much council housing, so renting is difficult. Buying can be nearly impossible. Remote and idyllic villages like Plockton (Ross & Cromarty) have house prices close to urban levels and far beyond local earnings. Not surprisingly, this has made economic change all the more difficult. Resentment has spilled over into minor 'English out' campaigns against second homes, for some believe there is an unacceptable social cost in allowing rural Scotland to be plaything for the prosperous.

The region's continuing social problems are exemplified in the persistently high rates of alcoholism and male suicide. More constructively, a strong collective memory and powerful traditions of affirmative action are shown in the bitter but successful campaign against the Skye Bridge tolls (1995–2004) and in tenant buyouts of land from absentee owners of, for example, the Assynt estates (1993) and Island of Eigg (1997).

Distinctions between Highland and Lowland Scotland have become increasingly blurred, but for visitors and incomers alike there is still something self-contained and serious about the people of the north and west, and still a feel of the frontier about places like Ullapool, Lerwick, and Lochinver.

Chapter 5
Economy and environment

The agricultural millennia

There have been people in Europe for at least 50,000 years, and it seems likely that in earlier Palaeolithic periods when the climate was kind (prior to c. 25000 BC) nomadic bands from the sparse population may have moved about northern Britain. However, all traces of humanity were obliterated by the Ice Age that ended in Scotland roughly 10,000 years ago. Glaciation helped resettlement because, in a reversal of global warming, water became ice and sea levels dropped dramatically, creating causeways between Britain and the Continent and between Scotland and Ireland. Climate continued to improve in this Mesolithic period (up to c. 4000 BC) and trees, animals, and eventually people moved northwards.

Scotland may once again have had some human inhabitants as early as 8000 BC, but the earliest recorded settlement is of a group of hunters on the Isle of Rum dating to c. 7000 BC. Extensive settlement did not take place until after c. 6000 BC, however the colonists were clearly accomplished sailors as many archaeological remains are found in the Western Isles. By this stage, the relative simplicity of early hunters had given way to hunter-gatherers' extensive exploitation of environmental resources on land, river, and sea. Yet these were still nomads who moved seasonally and left limited archaeological remains, their few artefacts suggesting

that settlers came less from England than from Ireland and the
North Sea basin. The land divided and the sea united, as it was to
do for thousands of years.

From c. 4000 BC, hunter-gatherers became more or less
permanently settled farmers who cultivated crops, domesticated
animals, developed new technologies (including pottery), and left
evidence of sophisticated communal cultures and belief systems.
This Neolithic age (up to c. 2500 BC) overlapped with the
Mesolithic and for thousands of years, thanks partly to the
abundance of resources, people adapted more or less peacefully to
migrations and to changes in climate and technologies and the
lifestyles they brought.

Dark Age Scotland may not have been as poor as it later became.
Treasure troves found by archaeologists, and the fact that both
southern kings and Scandinavians thought it worth plundering,
suggest otherwise. The same is true of the late Middle Ages and,
except when decimated by disease or warfare (as in the early 14th
century), population remained steady until demographic increase
and bad weather created widespread famines in the late 16th and
17th centuries. Pre-modern economies were just as fragile as
modern capitalism. The 1640s and 1650s were economically
disastrous for Scotland as war disrupted trade, bad harvests
created misery, and plague purged populations. Black-market
lenders charged interest rates of 15–20% unprecedented until the
1970s. The late 1690s saw starvation, population displacement,
and mortality from disease.

For centuries, Scottish agriculture mixed arable and pastoral
farming, depending on geography, soil, and climate. There was
some specialization – cattle- and sheep-raising in upland areas,
grain production in the lowlands – but it was not until the 17th
century that the Lothians began to witness major agrarian change
in response to Dutch examples and growing demand from

Edinburgh. Tenant numbers were reduced and farm sizes rose; field systems were reorganized from intermixed strips (*runrig*) to consolidated holdings; and new techniques of manuring, liming, and crop rotation made soil more fertile. After c. 1750, other areas of Lowland Scotland quickly followed.

The century 1750 to 1850 is usually called an age of agricultural 'improvement', both by its contemporary exponents and by later historians. The changes created the ordered modern landscape of fields, lanes, and substantial farmhouses, the necessary precursors of vastly improved agricultural output. Thanks to mechanization, it now takes less than one 'man-day' per year to tend an acre of barley compared with 22 in 1840 – when Lowland agriculture led the world. Agricultural improvement and economic diversification into trade and industry saw Scotland's population increasingly urbanized from 1750. Just 3% of Scots lived in large towns in 1650, but 30% in 1841. One-quarter worked in agriculture in 1841, 10% by 1911, and a mere 1% today.

Industrialization

Scotland had industry before the 18th century. Industrial sites existed in the Neolithic period, making stone axes, for example (though these were also imported from northern Ireland). Iron Age people were the first to exploit mineral resources for industry, but coal-mining took off only in the 16th century, using indentured miners whose status was close to serfs. Early coal production in the Lothians and Fife went to domestic hearths and to boil off sea water to make salt, but output expanded rapidly in the 18th century. From a few hundred tons a year c. 1700, Fife coal production alone surged to nearly 10 million tons a year in 1913. Until the 19th century, most other manufacturing was dispersed, small-scale 'cottage industry', using simple tools to process organic, agriculturally derived raw materials like wood, skin, hair, or plants.

Native manufacturing was slow to develop prior to c. 1780, but Scots had for centuries had economic interests in many such enterprises abroad and economic achievement also came through complete infiltration of other peoples' commerce (notably in Scandinavia and the Baltic), anticipating the role of later countrymen within the post-1707 British Empire. Yet there was domestic industry and trade: in the late 17th century dozens of new market centres were founded across the Lowlands and as many as one-third of the population may have had a non-agricultural job like making textiles, admittedly often part-time. There were concentrated enterprises like mines, shipyards, and the Carron Ironworks (Stirlings.) in the 18th century, but factories were not really a feature of industry until after the 1820s.

With basic industries and extensive, sophisticated European trade ties, the Scots would have managed economically during the 18th century, as they had for centuries before, but it is inconceivable that they would have done so well without access to England's colonial and domestic markets after the 1707 Union. A major winner was Glasgow, its 18th-century prosperity founded on tobacco and other colonially sourced groceries like sugar, which had changed from luxury to mass-market commodities during the 17th century. Only the 11th richest Scottish town in 1560, it was second to Edinburgh in 1660 (then still by far the wealthiest city) and it has been larger since the mid-18th century, now numbering 650,000 to Edinburgh's 450,000. Made by colonial trade like Bristol or Liverpool, Glasgow did not, like them, participate in the slave trade, though there were Scots slavers operating out of England and Scottish slave owners in the southern colonies and the Caribbean.

From the Middle Ages, towns like Glasgow existed to make things, to buy and sell, and to provide services. On the east coast, Dundee illustrates the changing economy of another major city. Second in size to Edinburgh in the Middle Ages (it was one of 52 royal burghs in 1296), it traded and sailed, with fishing and whaling feeding into shipbuilding: Scott of the Antarctic's vessel *Discovery* was launched there in 1901. Linen manufacturing in the 18th century was followed by jute (a hemp-like fibre from India) in the 19th. Fruit processing and publishing were also important industries in the 19th and 20th centuries. Dundee in the 19th-century was a proud and successful city with fine public architecture. Employment opportunities were skewed towards women (three-quarters of jute workers were female) and jobs for men often took them away from home, making Dundee a 'female' town that spawned a strong suffragette movement.

More normally, women were expected to take up any slack when demand for labour was buoyant and to make way for a man when it was not. Yet they were important industrial workers long before factories: for every male weaver of the 17th or 18th century, three or four women and children were employed preparing the raw materials for textiles. About one-third of Scottish women did paid work in 1901, but the proportion of married women in remunerated employment was half that of England. Men took their role as breadwinner seriously and employment was an important part of masculine identity. As late as the 1970s, women were still expected to stop paid work when they married.

Industrial work for women was mostly in textiles, centred in Lanarkshire, Renfrewshire, and the north-east Lowlands, while heavy industry such as iron and steel works and shipbuilding concentrated in and around Glasgow in the 19th century. The chemical complex at St Rollox in Glasgow was the largest manufactory in the world, while the merger of the thread-making firms of J. & P. Coats and Clarks of Paisley in 1896 created the largest manufacturing firm in Britain (and fifth largest in the world). For two centuries from c. 1760, Clyde shipbuilding epitomized Scotland's industrial success, and the yards were collectively the world's biggest in 1914.

9. The Forth Railway Bridge is the most recognizable icon of modern Scotland and an example of its remarkable 19th-century industrial success

By 1911, Scotland's economy resembled that of the rest of Britain, mixing industrial, textile, and service industries. Despite comprising only 10% of Britain's GDP, the first years of the 20th century marked the zenith of power and influence of Scottish capitalists, who controlled the biggest concentration of heavy industry in Britain and exerted substantial political influence. Their wealth, nestling in a separate Scottish banking system, enabled them to invest in shipping lines, railway companies, mining ventures, and vast expanses of farmland in North and South America, Australia, and South Africa. Alliance Trust, a Dundee-based investment trust founded in 1888 to channel funds into developing Australian and North American infrastructure, is currently Britain's largest such investment vehicle. Within Scotland, the Forth Railway Bridge was opened in 1890 and remains the country's most internationally recognized icon.

At no time before or since had Scotland been so closely integrated into the power structures of the empire it had helped to make and run as it was prior to World War I. At no time had it been so economically important. The society was peaceful. But there remained problems. Scotland had some of the worst slums in Britain. Social alignments and political allegiances were changing too. The stability produced by industrial expansion and benevolent paternalism was being replaced by the tensions of class. Coupled with a harsher economic climate after World War I, these forces would create a very different 20th-century Scotland.

Environment

It is a myth that pre-industrial people were more environmentally aware than post-industrial. True, until the widespread use of coal, energy came mainly from water, wood, or the muscles of people and animals, and was thus largely 'renewable'. So did most industrial raw materials until extensive exploitation of mineral resources in the 19th century. But the truth is that people worked with their environment because they did not have the means to tame it. They freely dumped domestic and industrial waste: water closets, introduced to middle-class homes in growing numbers from c. 1800, discharged into the street to end up in someone else's back-yard or in rivers, which were used as sewers or dumps as well as sources of water. Noxious substances used in and created by early industrial processes were left to scour the landscape and destroy the health of those who worked with them.

People exploited resources to their limit. The rich had gardens or 'policies' decorated with plants, and in the early cities there were 'physic' or medicinal herb gardens, but everyone else used the land for whatever food it could generate. The only reason they did not fish out the seas is because they lacked the technology. What 9,000 sailing boats caught in the 19th century can now be taken from the sea by three dozen trawlers. Convenient forests were exploited to make charcoal for iron smelting until the land was stripped bare, as happened around the Bonawe works at Taynuilt (Argylls.), though more usually woodland was closely managed, because timber was a valuable commodity and scarce even in the Middle Ages, as much clearance had been done by earlier farmers.

The wooded pre-modern environment was more biodiverse than it is now and richer in wildlife, but many apparently timeless features of Scotland's natural life are relatively recent. Heather only spread to the Cheviots in the 13th century, and for the last 200 years it has been on the decline across Scotland thanks to sheep grazing and forestry projects, though it still occupies 10% of the land area. For comparison, just 3% is now covered by towns, and woodlands make up 14%. Climatic change and the introduction of large numbers of livestock to the Highlands in the mid-19th century created a habitat which turned midges from an occasional into a persistent nuisance.

Environmental awareness and management has improved immeasurably in recent years, with changing sensibilities reflected in and guided by Scottish, British, and EU legislation. Mankind's recent attempts to harness nature to provide renewable energy have produced mixed results for the landscape. Nobody thinks twice about hydro-electric projects like Cruachan (Argylls., 1965), that use a controlled flow of water from a high loch to a lower one to power turbines – then pump it back up using off-peak electricity. Nuclear is another issue. Torness nuclear power station (1988) to the east of Edinburgh might be carbon-neutral, but it is also a monstrosity only too visible from the east-coast main road and train line – near the equally hideous Cockenzie coal-powered station (1967). The only other functioning nuclear plant in Scotland is Hunterston (Ayrs., 1976). Dounreay (Caithness, 1966), built when technology really was white-hot, closed in 1998. At least it was away from population, though the Norwegians might disagree. Opinion is divided on another energy artefact in the landscape – wind farms. Dating from the late 1990s, some see in them the majestic and environmentally friendly, others the noisy and out-of-place. A wave power plant is due to be constructed off Orkney in 2008–9.

Post-industrialization

Scots had supported free trade since the 17th century, but for much of the 20th century market capitalism's benefits for Scotland were elusive. In the short term, World War I favoured the heavy industries in which Scotland excelled, but demand for coal, steel, manufactures, and textiles dried up in the 1920s and 1930s, creating mass unemployment of up to 25% for the first time. The empire that had created markets began to compete in providing both raw materials like wool and finished products like jute. Scotland lost heavy industry and services like banks to the south and it could not attract new light industries such as car-making, chemicals, or consumer goods. The north–south divide in Britain was at its starkest during the Great Depression (1929–36).

Scotland's industry was never the same afterwards. Post-war Britain's people had enormous faith in the power of the state. Social infrastructure was indeed dramatically improved by the welfare state, with centrally planned government intervention profoundly changing the relationship between state and society. However, attempts to direct the post-war economy were much less successful. Prestige projects, such as the Linwood car plant (West Lothian), were brought to Scotland for political reasons, but demand for consumer products remained low and attempts to diversify the economy were no more successful than between the wars. Widespread ownership of domestic 'white goods' like televisions, vacuum cleaners, and washing machines did not come until the 1960s and they were mostly imports. Overseas competition during the 1960s signalled the onset of deep economic malaise and the launch of the liner *Queen Elizabeth II* on the Clyde in 1967 was a postscript to a proud industrial past. After two centuries centred on Glasgow, Scotland's economic focus began to shift back to Edinburgh.

Structural economic problems persisted and the last of Scotland's traditional industry disappeared in the 1980s. It now has no working coal mines. Yet modern Scotland is an economic success thanks to financial services, high-tech industries, and tourism/leisure. Employing 20% of the labour force, financial services (banking, fund management, pensions, and insurance) build on a long tradition. Some of the richest men of the 17th century were moneylenders, like goldsmith George Heriot, founder of the eponymous Edinburgh school. Scotland's currency was different until the use of sterling became widespread in the 18th century, when a Scots pound (just one of many currencies then in use) had slumped from rough parity in the Middle Ages to one-twelfth of a pound sterling. The financial model for the creation of the Bank of England in 1694 was Dutch, though tweaked by a Scotsman, William Paterson.

Scotland's own banking system was 'free' in the sense that it had no lender of last resort: competition between the Bank of Scotland (1695), the Royal Bank (1727), and other subsequent foundations delivering a more or less stable monetary environment until legislation in 1845 created much closer regulation. Scottish banks issued their own banknotes and, alongside those in Northern Ireland, still do. Frowned upon by some Londoners and most foreign exchange bureaux, these are worth exactly the same as a Bank of England note.

Scots inventors Alexander Graham Bell (1847–1922) – the telephone – and John Logie Baird (1888–1946) – the television – together made the modern computer age possible. During the 1970s and 1980s, electronics was a successful sector of the Scottish economy, with the long-established presence of IBM and Hewlett Packard as part of 'Silicon Glen' (not a place, simply a nickname for high-tech industries in Scotland). Yet its future is uncertain. When Timex withdrew in the early 1990s, Dundee's fortunes slumped; NCR is still there (making cash registers), but retrenching. Computing is the world's largest industry and there are innovative specialist electronic companies, Scotland currently excelling more in areas such as biotechnology and software development than the hardware side of high-tech. Dundee is now reviving on the back of digital media companies.

Though subject to the vagaries of weather (some Scots ironically quip that global warming is no bad thing), the fluctuating US dollar, and fear of terrorism, tourism flourishes, especially in historic towns and for outdoor activities such as golf, sailing, climbing, hill-walking, and scuba diving. The service sector as a whole has been the success story of the last generation. After all, one can buy televisions and trainers manufactured in China, but it is hard to out-source a haircut or an order of haddock and chips to India. Whisky production accounts for just 2% of Scottish employment, but it is Scotland's most valuable export and ranks fifth among UK export-earning manufactures.

Chapter 6
Scotland and the wider world

Scots and English

Scots–English enmity is a fact of life, but it is not inherent. As Chapter 1 showed, Dark Age Britain was politically and socially fluid. Dynastic alliances and 'Normanization' might have created greater unity in the Middle Ages. Indeed, the English only started seeing the Scots (and the Irish and Welsh) as barbarous and alien in the 12th century, Lowlanders perceived Highlanders as different from the 14th century (and vice versa), and a settled Anglophobia is clear among Scots by 1400. Thereafter, tensions were never far beneath the surface of Scots–English relationships.

While the Norman kings of England might sometimes treat the Scots shabbily, it was the Wars of Independence that really soured relations. Strictly speaking, the wars only lasted until 1328, but conflict continued viciously if intermittently until 1560, creating a legacy of distrust, double-dealing, broken promises, and betrayal that continues to invigorate relations between Scotland and England today. Edward I set the ball rolling. Installations of Scottish kings (proper coronations from 1329) were held at Scone (Perths.). Among other vandalism, Edward removed the 'Stone of Destiny' from Scone, hoping to appropriate a symbol of the antiquity and lineage of Scotland's kings. They stood rather than sat on it, making bizarre its placement like a commode under the coronation throne in Westminster Abbey until, in 1996, it was given back in a sad attempt to protect Tory seats in Scotland.

Later English kings managed effortlessly to build on Edward's legacy, and as early as 1348 a chronicler told how the Scots rejoiced as the English died in droves from the plague, while in 1435 a traveller remarked: 'nothing pleases the Scots more than abuse of the English'. In 1400, Henry IV took an army to Edinburgh in a lame attempt to press his claim as overlord of Scotland, but was politely sent home. Edward IV (1461–83) and Henry VII (1485–1509) were more diplomatic: Henry concluded a 'perpetual peace' in 1502 and married his daughter Margaret to James IV, enabling the Union of the Crowns in 1603.

Over time, English kings came to recognize that Scotland could not be conquered and that England was only one of its concerns, though they never really accepted the independence that this implied. For their part, medieval Scottish chronicles set Scotland in the context of European and Middle Eastern history and there were long periods when Scotland's political nation seemed indifferent to their neighbour.

With grandiose imperial ambitions and a belief in Scotland's dynastic dependency, Henry VIII pushed much harder than his father Henry VII. Plans to marry James V's infant daughter Mary, Queen of Scots, to Henry's son Edward were scuppered by the shrewd diplomacy of her mother, Mary of Guise, following James's death in 1542 after the Battle of Solway Moss. Henry's subsequent touch was none too subtle: a 'rough wooing' that included damaging attacks on southern Scotland.

By then, there was no going back in relations between the peoples. The claim that God himself was English comes from a self-boosting text of 1559 that warned the English to 'fear neither French nor Scots'. Even when aided by English playwright William Shakespeare, who made the Scots in 'Macbeth' (c. 1605–6) as noble and courtly as the English, James VI/I's hope that the Scots would forget the arrogance of the English to create a union 'with ane universall unanimitie of hairtis' ignored centuries of history.

Institutionalized discrimination and casual racism touched the Scots in England. Some lawyers were optimistic enough to claim English citizenship for Scots, but Henry VII passed an act in 1492 to deport non-naturalized Scots from England. Borderers felt ambivalent about the neighbours because of centuries of raiding. Wrongly calling someone a Scot was actionable in the 15th-century north of England, and Newcastle's guilds flatly refused to accept Scottish apprentices.

As economic migrants, later Scots were patronized or vilified in the popular art and literature of 18th-century London, when cartoons parodying the manners and aspirations of parsimonious and parochial Scots-on-the-make set the tone for 19th- and 20th-century media stereotypes. The Scottish surgeons who sought work in 18th-century London were 'like flocks of vultures' to one disaffected observer, while philosopher David Hume and his contemporary the Earl of Bute, George III's erstwhile tutor and a leading politician of the 1760s, personally felt the anti-Scottish sentiment there. Scottish MPs and peers were described, in terms that might secretly please their modern equivalents, as 'very fit for business, intriguing, cunning, tricking sort of men'. Even when contributing to it, Scots continued to feel estranged from English society, yet aware that cultural models, economic opportunities, and political focus lay there.

Cultural influences

Historic Scots, like their modern successors, thought about England only when they had to. For centuries, there was the whole of Europe to consider: from the papacy in Rome, to trade with the Baltic and Low Countries, to education and diplomacy in France. English influence there was, but until the 18th century it was only one of many, and in important areas like education, law, and religion it was among the least significant. From then there was a world empire too.

Europe offered Scotland an enduring alternative focus for warfare and diplomacy, commerce, and culture. The 'Auld Alliance' with France offered military support against England, though it rested on a much older Anglo-Norman presence: in 1212, the Scottish court was described as 'French in race and manner of life, in speech and in culture' – as were many courts from Burgos to Jerusalem. English kings who wanted to pursue claims to French territory (as they did until the 16th century) had to think twice about Scottish raids. Scottish soldiers fought with the French against the English in the 15th century and in Protestant armies in the wars that ravaged continental Europe from 1618 to 1648.

Medieval Scots wool went to Bruges (modern Belgium), then part of Burgundy, which supplied James II's queen, Mary of Gueldres, and two huge siege canons, one of which, 'Mons Meg', still points out from Edinburgh castle. Scots in the 16th and 17th centuries traded across the Baltic and North Sea, but notably with Veere and Rotterdam in the Low Countries, where they exchanged raw materials for specialist manufactures, including Delftware and Dutch paintings. Europe's universities contributed to the development of Scottish culture. Edinburgh's Botanic Gardens were founded by Sir Robert Sibbald on the model of Leiden's 'physic' gardens (1667), and Dutch training led to the flourishing Scottish medical schools of the 18th century.

Scotland was hardly a major player, but Scottish Renaissance kings were supposed to be cultured and James I had the reputation of an accomplished archer, musician, and poet, best known for the 'Kingis Quair'. Later monarchs cut a figure on the European stage by cockiness, careful diplomacy, and a feel for the right modes and fashions in culture and architecture. Renaissance literary culture was largely advisory and political, and when James III composed poetry, or James V commissioned it from Buchanan and Sir David Lindsay, or when James VI wrote about government, each was being cultured, but each was also using the culture of his court to act a political part. For the same reasons, all Stewart monarchs patronized Italian, French, and English musicians.

From the Middle Ages, examples of Continental architectural styles enriched Scotland's built environment. English perpendicular architecture is almost unknown in late medieval Scottish churches and the strongest analogies are with the French 'flamboyant' style. Romanesque-looking architectural features of the 14th–16th century are found at four important ecclesiastical centres, Aberdeen, Dunkeld, St Andrews, and Dunfermline. This assertive Scottish Romanesque revival heralded the reception of Italian Renaissance architectural motifs. Linlithgow Palace, begun by James I in 1425 and extended by James III and James IV, was

In folchem Habit Gehen die 800 In Stettin angekommen Irrlander oder Irren.

10. The Scots were always a migratory people, here depicted as soldiers fighting for Sweden in northern Germany during the Thirty Years War, 1618–48 (though wrongly labelled Irish in The German caption). The image shows the ways in which a 'plaid', or bolt of cloth, could be worn

modelled on Italian seignorial palaces such as the Palazzo Venezia, and other lavish projects included the Palace Block at Stirling Castle and Falkland Palace (both early 16th century). Dutch-influenced crow-stepped gables characterize vernacular architecture from the 15th to 17th centuries, notably in Fife fishing villages from Culross to Crail.

Emigration

'Rats, lice and Scotsmen: you find them everywhere', or so a medieval French proverb ran. Against the usual preconception that people were born, lived, and died within sight of their parish church prior to industrialization and the railways (as they really did in France), the Scots were a highly mobile people from an early date. Half the population of an 18th-century parish might move elsewhere within a generation, to be replaced by incomers, thanks to insecure land tenure, sometimes restricted economic opportunities, a poor relief system where the able-bodied unemployed struggled to get help, and mobility of the young to work as domestic and agricultural servants (which is how most people spent their teens prior to the 20th century). Moving home or job was quite normal, so for many emigration was not a wrench.

As the proverb suggests, Scottish emigration was an established fact from the 13th century, and by the 17th century, Scots can be found in Scandinavia and the Baltic (including Russia), the Low Countries, and Iberia, as well as France. Some were traders, other soldiers and sailors, a few were students. Temporary and permanent, much of the movement was by individuals. Most were young men, helping to explain why for centuries the age at first marriage for women was so late. Some were families, but organized mobility only took off in the 17th century.

The first example, the plantation of Ulster (1609–41), was a piece of social engineering carried out by English and Scottish 'undertakers': landed proprietors who undertook to people their assigned lands with tenants well affected to crown and Protestantism. Late 17th-century Scots immigrants were mostly industrious, intent Presbyterians fleeing persecution, their beliefs squaring them not only against native Irish Catholics, but also members of the Anglican Church of Ireland: an enduringly bitter cocktail. More 17th-century Scots probably went to the Baltic, but the long-term political legacy of their presence in Ulster is far weightier than mere numbers because of the distinctive way incomers there perceived their religious and social mission. Others started to move to the North American (New Jersey and South Carolina) and Caribbean colonies, especially from the end of the 17th century, though English emigration to America was far greater.

Scottish emigration gathered pace in the 18th century. Some 60,000 emigrated voluntarily 1700–80, but not all movers had a choice. There was a white slave trade in children as young as 9 or 10, kidnapped from the alleys of 17th-century Aberdeen for sale in Virginia; 100,000 young children, by no means all orphans, were shipped to Canada c. 1870–1920; and as late as the 1960s, forcible emigration to Australia was a way of dealing with orphans and children of the destitute. Australia was also a dumping ground for transported convicts, 1776–1857.

Better-known injustices than the child trade are the 19th-century clearances of population, notably the sometimes tragic tale of the Highlands discussed earlier. Yet forcible clearance of the Highlands is only part of the story. Late 18th- and early 19th-century Highland migration was often peasant-led, with landowners keen to prevent movement: a sort of 'people's clearance'. And if one sort of migrant came from those dispossessed by the Highland clearances, Lowland (disproportionately urban and industrial) emigration was every bit as significant as Highland (rural agrarian). Here the outflow was not from some backward, agrarian society like that of Norway or Portugal, but a dynamic, modern economy that may nevertheless have shed two million people c. 1800–1939. The majority went to North America (28% to Canada, 44% to the USA) and 25% to the Antipodes. Roughly half a million Scots emigrated to Australia 1781–1987.

Victorian emigrants from Scotland, whose population drain was second only to Ireland in Europe, were thus as likely to be voluntary exiles from a vital, industrializing, and urbanizing society with an improving standard of living – which attracted substantial Irish immigration. Literate, skilled, and motivated, Scotland exported what were often its best. Scots had been important in making North America, with tobacco traders and other merchants in the major towns of the eastern seaboard. Prior to 1850, nearly all British doctors and many clergymen in North America (and anywhere else) were either Scots or Scottish trained; Scottish educators too flourished at Princeton and Philadelphia. Emigrant industrialists helped modernize and develop foreign economies, notably Thomas Glover (1838–1911) in Japan and Andrew Carnegie (1835–1919) in the USA. Emigration was again particularly rapid in the 1920s, 1930s, and 1960s. In an age of national angst, the poet Edwin Muir (1887–1959) saw the 1930s as a 'silent clearance'. Scottish emigration rates are currently still the highest in the UK, this from a demonstrably successful modern economy.

While Scots in Ulster strove for Union and a Protestant homeland, its emigrants elsewhere did not, preferring to make their way by 'fitting in'. For example, Scots and Scots-Irish (or rather Scots-British) became Americans, Catholic-Irish became Irish-Americans, retaining an identity and lending powerful support for Irish nationalism. Scots abroad form an ethnic category, loosely incorporated by sense of history and perceived difference with outsiders. They also constitute an ethnic association, with social and sometimes political organization to express shared aims, but not an ethnic community that has a clear national, territorial reference point (like the Irish), however sympathetic the countless millions of Scots descent currently living worldwide feel towards their ancestral homeland (such feelings are strongest in former 'white' colonies). Scots fit in and, perhaps for that reason, the world likes them.

Well, maybe not all the world. There are now nearly 1.2 million Scots-born inhabitants of England, and they and Scottish visitors are sometimes subject to the casual racism of 'pet' names like 'Jock' (John, rather than a sporty type) and routine references to haggis, whisky, and kilts that would provoke outcry if directed against the supposed cultural icons of other minorities. Identifying modern Scots (or Irish) by the alleged characteristics of their possibly Celtic ancestors – such as love of alcohol or fighting – is merely an extension of 19th-century racist stereotyping.

This apparently trivial condescension highlights how some English are in two minds about the Scots, accepting them as fellow Britons while still seeing them as different and even perhaps as an annoyance. Scots may feel the same about the English (see below). English ambivalence explains why former PM Tony Blair (1997–2007), born and raised in Edinburgh, once refused to answer directly when asked if he thought himself Scottish, for to say so could have been politically damaging. Current PM Gordon Brown, more obviously a Scot (brought up in Kirkcaldy, Fife), might sometimes like to do the same.

Empire

Scots peopled, and many helped to run, the British Empire of the 18th and 19th centuries. But Scotland's first imperial experiences were on the receiving end. The Romans, wisdom has it, brought civilization to northern Europe: towns, roads, literacy, art, and baths. In the words of the famous spoof history of England, *1066 and all that* (1930): 'The Roman Conquest was ... a *Good Thing*, since the Britons were only natives at that time.' Yet Roman Britain was as populated as Stewart Britain and there was sophisticated agriculture, industry, government, and communications long before the Romans, who labelled the inhabitants of Britain barbarians for their own purposes. Robust native societies, economies, and political systems may explain why many cultural aspects of Roman rule, such as their religion, never took hold. Latin persisted only among the learned, though it enriched all vocabularies. There was also a tangible legacy of buildings, roads, and boundaries in the landscape and the vaguer, but still important, experience of integration into Europe-wide political and economic networks.

The colonized peoples, experiencing what the Romans did *to* rather than *for* them, endured 350 years of expropriation, exploitation, and military occupation. The Romans tore apart pre-existing political institutions to create a top-down imperial machine, sacrificing the development of indigenous peoples to Roman needs. Ardoch fort (Perths.) housed 20,000 soldiers in the 2nd century, and the campaigns of Septimius Severus against the Maeatae and the Caledonians of the eastern Lowlands in the early 3rd century involved rampaging armies of perhaps 50,000 men – numbers without precedent before or since on British soil.

The second imperial experience was at the hands of the Norsemen and from aspirant Northumbrian and then English monarchs. As early as the 10th century, kings of England liked to claim rule over 'all other peoples living in the ambit of the British island'. The Normans too had aspirations, better realized by indirect influence than the heavy-handed efforts at imposition by Edward I and his successors. 'Empire' for the English meant domination of Britain (and preferably of France too) right up to the 16th century, though after the Wars of Independence English attacks were more to punish or to pre-empt a Scottish threat than serious attempts to conquer the country.

From James III onwards, Scots monarchs too made explicitly imperial claims of extension and consolidation. One implication was facing up to their internal colonial problem and they used policy, propaganda, and force to assimilate, pacify, and 'civilize' a Gaelic-speaking clan society tainted with what the Statutes of Iona termed in 1609 'barbarity and incivility'. Only in the 18th century was the 'British Empire' redefined ideologically to stress not the dominance of one part over another, but a shared enterprise or common wealth, yet that identity was partly achieved by the unremitting project to 'civilize' the Highlands.

After the collapse of their own overseas-empire-building project in Panama, Scots participated eagerly in Britain's world empire and revelled in its benefits. They owned much of the land on Grenada and Jamaica in the mid-18th century. One-ninth of civil servants and one-third of army officers in late 18th-century India were Scots. The rousing anthem 'Rule Britannia' was composed by the Anglo-Scot James Thomson in 1740. The British Empire encompassed one-quarter of the human race in 1914, when young Scotsmen flocked to defend it against Germany (27% of adult males fought; 100,000 never came back), and Scotland's 19th-century industrial and commercial success is unthinkable without it.

Like the Romans in Britain, empire brought good and bad to indigenous peoples abroad. On the plus side were communications, administrative and governmental structures, formalized law codes, education, and (arguably) the English language itself. More negatively, famines, taxes, lies, looting, land-grabbing, and the opium trade cannot be forgotten, especially after the mid-19th century. All types of colonialism rearranged indigenous politics, economics, and social relationships to suit the political, military, and economic needs of the colonizer, distorting existing structures in ways still felt today. Genocide, torture, and sexual humiliation were among the tools of the British Empire. The punishment for slave rebellion on Jamaica was 'nailing them on the ground with crooked Sticks on every Limb, and then applying the Fire by degrees to the Feet and Hands, burning them

gradually up to the Head, whereby their pains are extravagant'.
Untrammelled by modern notions of political correctness,
resourceful Scots used any means to gain commercial advantage,
including 'connubial alliances' between men from Orkney and
native women in Canada's Hudson's Bay. The part played by
distinctively Scottish ideas, both religious and political, in
softening the impact of colonialism, and eventually in encouraging
a retreat from empire, cannot disguise this darker side.

Modern observers may be uneasy about the age of empire, even
while Britain still engages in post-imperial projects with the USA.
Few now subscribe to the glorification of early 20th-century
Scottish novelist John Buchan's ripping militaristic and
imperialist yarns, characterized by what modern readers would
see as jaw-dropping political incorrectness. Yet even when
troubled by post-colonial guilt, it is hard not to respect the
optimism, enterprise, and tenacity of those who left Scotland's
shores. Many probably expected to come home and one-third of
late 19th-century emigrants did, but in some parts of the empire
more than half died from violence or disease – the 18th-century
Caribbean and India at any time were particularly unhealthy.

Nor can we ignore the intense pride Scots felt in their role, both
while abroad and at home: the empire was taught in schools to
show Scotland's part in the United Kingdom, and Victorian
Glasgow trumpeted itself as 'the second city of empire'. Voluntary
bodies like the Boys Brigade, founded in Glasgow in 1883,
promoted Christian values and celebrated imperial achievements.
Extending the connection between monarchy and militarism,
pride in Scottish regiments overseas was also an important part
of identity.

Immigration and cultural pluralism

Scotland has been a net exporter of people for centuries and
emigration was only counterbalanced by limited inward

movement, including a handful of Scandinavians, Eastern Europeans, Dutch, English, and French. All pre-19th-century immigration was small-scale and it was the Irish who were the first significant group: one in fifteen of Scotland's population was Irish-born in 1871, one in ten by 1901, with a strong presence in greater Glasgow, Edinburgh, and Dundee. Some immigrants were Ulster Protestants, but most were Catholic Irish, who did not assimilate, living in certain (poor) quarters of towns and rarely inter-marrying with native Scots, from whose antipathy they suffered for their race, religion, and espousal of Irish nationalism.

Having ebbed and flowed since the Reformation, sectarianism was at its strongest between the 1820s and 1930s and is now fading, seemingly confined to the tribalism of football matches between Glasgow Rangers (historically Protestant since it moved to Ibrox in 1899) and Celtic (historically Catholic). In its day, it was a powerful and ugly force on both sides, based on visceral fear and dislike. Seeing it as an anti-Protestant, anti-British fifth column, Protestant Orange Lodges were dedicated to discriminating against and aiming to extinguish Catholicism, mixing religious antagonism with racism against Highlanders and Irish alike.

The existence since the 17th century of English-born people in Scotland is less well known, yet by 1921 they had replaced the Irish as the largest migrant group and are currently one-twelfth of the total population (fully one-fifth of those living in southern Scotland). The modern image of the English in Scotland is of the counter-urban 'white settler', allegedly leaving a six-figure salary and a seven-figure house in London for a quiet life on a Scottish Highland estate. The reality is that, past and present, most have come to work, mainly in manual and, more recently, managerial jobs.

Incomers from England are still sometimes the butt of jibes about their origins, treated not as other foreigners, but as English. Yet they are generally accepted and they come to appreciate what it means to be Scottish: the sense of history (including the political and cultural shadow cast by England); the feeling of social equality, civic trust, and civic compassion; the independently minded, open, and sincere people. English expatriates in Scotland may become more Scottish than the Scots, shouting themselves hoarse for their adopted country at sporting internationals. More in paternalism than empathy, even the native English will adopt Scotland (or Ireland) at sporting contests when their own side is not playing. Most Scots (or Irish) would sooner die than reciprocate. English anywhere are usually happy to play the Scottish card if they have a suitable ancestor, whatever their ambivalence about the Scots.

Other immigrant groups have enriched Scottish society over time, including Italians and Jews fleeing poverty and persecution in the 1890s and 1900s. Carrying on a tradition that lasted from the Middle Ages through World War II, the most prominent current immigrants are Eastern or 'new' Europeans, usually filling the sorts of manual vacancies left by the falling birth rates and changing work preferences of indigenous Scots. Young people from across Europe and as far as Australia and New Zealand are also keen to live and work in Scotland.

Minorities identifiable by sight rather than sound are uncommon in Scotland and always were. Apart from working as personal servants, black men served in British ships and regiments until the mid-19th century, when the new racism pushed them out. Until the 20th century, non-whites living in Scotland were numbered in hundreds and even New Commonwealth immigration was small: Scotland had about 600 Asians in 1950 and 4,000 in 1960. Currently less than 2% of Scotland's population is non-white and 'cultural pluralism' is much less of a colour issue than in England, which has 10% non-whites.

Intolerance remains, perhaps because minorities are both few and relatively silent. Gratuitous anti-Semitism and thoughtless racism – like 'Chinky' for Chinese meal – are disappearing, though some see these being replaced by Islamophobia. Other minorities, such as Travellers, are becoming accepted. Yet the pursuit of equality within diversity has obstacles to overcome. In 2000, Brian Souter, who founded the thriving transport company Stagecoach with his sister Anne Gloag, led a vigorous and popular (and partly successful) campaign against the repeal of legislation banning the promotion of homosexuality (only de-criminalized in Scotland in 1980). Scots increasingly accept that minorities can pursue alternative lifestyles in private, but they reserve the right to regard some such choices as morally wrong for the public.

Chapter 7
Culture

Language

A Celtic language called 'British' was spoken in Britain at the time
of the Roman conquest. From this descended modern Welsh,
Cornish, and Breton languages. British became heavily influenced
by Latin during the Roman period, but remained essentially a
single language until at least 800 and the different daughter
languages were probably largely intelligible until at least 1100. The
speakers of these languages were generally referred to as Britons
by themselves and their neighbours. 'British' was understood thus
until the Union of 1707 and the appropriation of the term for
something quite different led to a decline in the usage. 'Breton' as
an English word was coined only in the 19th century to replace the
by then confusing 'British'.

Pictish probably started out as a dialect of British, but escaped the
impact of Latin and retained important Celtic influences. Place
names and personal names suggest that all of Scotland was
British-speaking before the Anglo-Saxons, except for the west
coast from Kintyre north, which was Gaelic-speaking. The word
'aber' (as in Aberdeen) is the British word for a river mouth, as
opposed to Gaelic 'inver' (as in Inverness). Gaelic-speaking Scots
in the west may have spoken a Celtic language intelligible to
British-speaking Picts in the east, and early Scotland was probably

a linguistic as well as a political and ethnic melting pot. More distinctively, the Northern and Western Isles were mainly Norse-speaking between the 9th and 14th centuries, and there is a strong legacy of place names, but 'Norn' was all but gone from Orkney by 1600 and Shetland by 1800.

The Anglo-Norman nobility were most at home with French, though ordinary Scots became no more French-speaking than did the English, even if both vocabularies were enriched. Widespread English-speaking came to southern Scotland with the Angles (English incomers) from c. 600, but a more important influence was from English-speaking settlers of burghs from David I's reign onwards.

Thus Gaelic was never the only Scottish tongue, though in the 12th century it was the majority language. It has been in decline ever since: the first language of perhaps half of Scotland in 1400, one-third in 1689, but just one-fifth in 1806 and one-twelfth in 1900. In 1961, there were just 81,000 Gaelic speakers and 59,000 in 2001. Naked hostility explains some of the retreat, especially in the 17th and 18th centuries when Gaelic and a militaristic clan society became associated with a threat to the British political establishment. However, the most rapid contraction came in the 19th century after active proscription of any kind had ceased and when Gaelic was being helped by the first full Gaelic Bible (1801) and by published poetry collections.

The problem was that speaking Gaelic gave access to a rich heritage and culture, but not speaking English was an economic liability. The 1872 Education Act banned school lessons in Gaelic, but Highlanders were already won over to the benefits of English as a result of seasonal migration to the Lowlands for harvest work and imperial service in the British army. In 1904, it became possible to learn Gaelic in school as a subject in its own right rather than as a means of acquiring English, but this reversal of centuries of proscription had little effect.

In modern Scotland, 1% of the population speak Gaelic, most of them living not in the Highlands and Islands, but in Glasgow, which has since the 1960s been as much the true centre of Gaeldom. Across Europe, the decline of 'lesser-used' languages has been halted as part of a new cultural preference for diversity. The London-based BBC is often accused of patronizing Scots. There is truth to this, but also irony, as the BBC's vision of educating and edifying the masses to create a morally cohesive British society, which still dominates 'public-service broadcasting', is that of a Scot, John Reith (1889–1971), the BBC's first director-general (1927). Yet the BBC is more accommodating to regional diversity than once it was. Through passionate advocates like journalist and broadcaster Lorn MacIntyre, BBC Scotland has helped breathe new life into Gaelic. The success of Gaelic rockers like Runrig and Capercaillie has done no harm either. In 2005, a Gaelic Language Act gave it 'equal respect'.

A dialect of English (a Germanic language, like Norse) and a tongue always subject to Anglicization, Scots (sometimes known as Doric or 'broad Scots') was never an important component of historic identity, though it was the language of government and law by c. 1500. At the time of the Reformation, Protestant leaders adopted English versions of the Geneva Bible and the Psalter and the English 'Form of Prayers' as the 'Book of Common Order'. The first authentically colloquial New Testament in Scots was not completed until two centuries after its Gaelic counterpart (four centuries after the Reformation) and was not published until 1983.

At a time when the 'enlightened' took lessons to extinguish Scoticisms, Scots' greatest exponent was Robert Burns, though he also wrote in English. Long dismissed as archaic, even embarrassing, and gradually eroded by post-Victorian universal education, Scots revived in the late 20th century and now has a vibrant print culture. Yet spoken Scots flourishes most strongly in modern Northern Ireland, where it has been aggressively marketed as a cultural counterweight in Unionism to the skilfully lobbied role of Gaelic in Irish nationalism.

A more obvious modern linguistic distinction is the way English is pronounced in parts of Scotland. Accents in the fishing communities of the north-east or eastern Fife can mystify visitors and are equally impenetrable to someone schooled in the windy canyons of Edinburgh's New Town. BBC television's 'Rab C. Nesbitt' (Gregor Fisher) offers an attenuated taste of broad Glaswegian accents (working-class – or rather unemployed – Govan in this case) – and deeper and more painful insights into the multiple deprivations of segments of modern Scottish society than many a po-faced documentary.

Festivals

Scotland is short on national calendar festivals and most public holidays were until recently localized. The Kirk sidelined Christmas and Easter. Christmas became a public holiday only in 1958, Boxing Day in 1974, and Easter is still less important than in England. However, the Yule festivities so proscribed were extremely popular and became displaced onto Hogmanay (31 December). As in England, modern Christmas is a Victorian reinvention with a new iconography of trees, cards, and crackers. For all its appeal to pope-burning Scots (though James VI/I warned that people should attack disloyalty, not Catholics), the anniversary of Guy Fawkes' attempt to blow up the London parliament (5 November 1605) was not widely celebrated in Scotland until the 1920s or 1930s, when unemployment and trumped-up scares about Irish immigration promoted renewed sectarian tensions and riots in Glasgow and Edinburgh. The more observant might also have noticed that one aim of the Gunpowder plotters was to get rid of Scottish hangers-on at James VI/I's new London court.

St Andrew's Day (30 November) is officially recognized, but better known is the unofficial celebration of Burns Day (25 January). Neither is a public holiday. The Burns Supper is one of the few invented traditions whose roots were contemporaneous with the event it celebrated. But in its first manifestation there was already the commercialism with which many such traditions have become associated. Even before his death, Burns' cottage in Alloway, Ayrshire, had been sold to the incorporation of shoemakers of Ayr, one of whose members turned it into an alehouse. It was here, on 29 January 1801 (they got his birthday wrong), that soldiers of the Argyll Fencibles (militia) met to hear their band play – and to use the services of his cottage in its new role. The first recorded Supper took place at Alloway in the same year, but on the anniversary of his death (21 July). It involved a speech and multiple toasts; to eat, there was haggis (which was addressed) and sheep's head; given the social status of those present, refreshment was probably wine and ale rather than whisky. Among celebrants was a lady, though thereafter the Suppers were mostly (sometimes militantly) all-male affairs until the 20th century. The 'toast to the lasses' was traditionally thanks for the cooking and an appreciation of the women in Burns' life, only later degenerating into a sexist (often misogynistic) rant. Celebrations were held twice yearly until 1809, when participants settled on 25 January, because this fell in a slack period of the agricultural year.

Most other major festivals are local or regional, reflecting the small-scale, devolved, community basis of life for much of Scotland's past. The major towns still have their own holiday periods, known as 'the trades' after the craft and trade organizations on which their prosperity was once built. Other examples include fairs like Lammas, a Celtic autumn festival commemorated on 1 August. It survives in Fife burghs, but as vulgar commercialized funfairs and markets shorn of their traditional functions of hiring (for which Martinmas on

11 November was also significant), hand-fasting (betrothal), and sociability. Border towns have 'Common Ridings' (of the marches) in June that look like survivals of historic boundary perambulations, but are in fact complex, living pageants that make powerful ritual statements about modern civic values. The classic academic study of sociologist James Littlejohn – *Westrigg* (1963), about life in a Borders farming community in the 1950s – charts the changing texture of the rural world's communal and personal relationships under pressure from modernization.

Most large-scale historic rituals had some political purpose, like the pre-1707 'riding' that opened parliament, a procession from Holyrood to the Parliament House west of St Giles (reproduced in 1999). Many cities' 19th-century rituals and galas also formed part of a carefully choreographed civic identity that gave substance to civil society.

Complete with Viking costumes and a burning longboat, the Shetland festival of Up-Helly-Aa (last Tuesday in January) looks like a Norse, pagan, Dark-Age relic, but actually started in the 17th century and reached recognizable form in the late 19th century. Thereafter, it was continually remodelled and reinvented to cope with the communal stresses of economic and social change – notably since oil exploration and extraction became major employers in the 1970s. Involving music, dancing, and trials of strength, Highland games or gatherings too were a 19th-century reinvention. The most famous is that now held at Braemar (Aberdeens.), started in 1815 as a mutual assistance society and given the royal imprimatur in 1866. Yet these games are a pale imitation of the feasting and fighting that had been the true sport of pre-modern Highlanders, when martial prowess and conspicuous consumption were important symbols of power and status.

The Edinburgh International Festival was first held in August 1947 to regenerate Scotland and reintegrate with Europe. For decades, it was a small affair that promoted elite, classical-music-centred tourism and was adored by cultural 'luvvies', but was never really accepted by the staid citizenry. Only since Edinburgh shook off its dowdy provincial image in the 1980s has it been embraced and flourished. The core event presently comprises a military pageant or 'tattoo', whose popularity is seemingly impervious to political correctness, an official festival of theatre, music, and dance, plus film and book components. Artists or companies have to apply for accreditation and a 'fringe' exists for the endless variety of performers (notably comedians in recent years) who do not attempt or who miss the cut. The city 'hoaches' or 'heaves' (is busy) with visitors and the air buzzes with performance.

Alongside its museums and art galleries, the Festival helped give Edinburgh a name for (high) culture, but Glasgow (which had an art academy from the 18th century) is a more vibrant design centre, notably for architecture, furniture, and textiles. It also has a better modern music scene and it is arguably at least as 'cultured'.

Art and architecture

Medieval monks produced beautifully illuminated manuscripts, but most of those described as 'painters' before the 18th century worked on heraldry or decorating noble ceilings, some churches, or coffins. Those who could afford paintings to hang up bought from the Netherlands, and when Charles II wanted a series of Scottish kings for Holyrood palace in the 1660s he went to Jacob de Witt. Fine native portrait painters flourished thereafter, of whom Allan Ramsay (1713–84) and Sir Henry Raeburn (1756–1823) are the best known. Concentrating on history, landscape, animals, and Highland sentiment, Scottish painting after David Allan (1744–96) and Sir David Wilkie (1785–1841) was mostly worthy, but romanticized, dull, and derivative.

Only late in the 19th century was it re-animated by 'the Glasgow boys' – a term used by the art establishment to disparage the likes

11. *The Wealth of Nations,* by Sir Eduardo Paolozzi. Located at South Gyle Business Park in Edinburgh, the statue borrows the title of Adam Smith's famous text on economics of 1776, but celebrates people and their imaginations

of Sir James Guthrie (1859–1930) and E. A. Hornel (1864–1933). The Glasgow boys inspired Colourists like Francis Cadell (1883–1937) and Samuel Peploe (1871–1935), who in turn carried Impressionism into the 1920s and 1930s. There was a revival of Scottish culture in this period, most notably poetry and the novels of Neil Gunn and Lewis Grassic Gibbon about the decay of historic communities; the National Trust for Scotland was founded in 1931. However, what was produced is more appreciated now than it was then. A more modern artist who did enjoy celebrity in his lifetime was Leith-born surrealist-turned-pop-artist Sir Eduardo Paolozzi (1924–2005), best known for muscular sculptures.

Scotland contains examples of all major European architectural styles from the last millennium. Many have been creatively adapted, others made distinctively new. Because wealth was concentrated in towns and among rural landowners, it is in urban architecture and in castles and country houses that the longest historical record can be found. With rare exceptions, such as the miraculously well-preserved Neolithic village at Skara Brae on Orkney, little except defensive structures have survived prior to the Middle Ages, though archaeologists are beginning to fill the gaps.

Skara Brae and the hundreds of small huts that once clustered around the British stronghold of Traprain Law (East Lothian) show that communal living was not universal before modern times. Privacy, however, was neither expected nor easy to come by. 'Crannogs' or artificial islands were built on lochs for defensive purposes c. 3000 BC to c. AD 1700, some with dwellings on stilts. Distinctively Scottish fortified circular towers called 'brochs' were built in numbers, mostly in the Iron Age, along the northern and western coasts, attesting the importance of the sea, the extent of wealth to be amassed, displayed, and protected, and the enduring threat from raiders.

From the 6th century (and probably before), much visual art was religious and churches are among the oldest buildings, though early churches and noble seats were often wooden and the modern return to masonry architecture occurred as late as 1100. Building materials were commonly recycled and little survives pre-1400 except remote ruins. From then on, churches grace town and country alike. There are ornate Renaissance jewels like Roslin Chapel (c. 1450), giving way after the Reformation to austere boxes like the Tron Kirk (1647) and Canongate Kirk (1691) in Edinburgh, the latter by James Smith, who also built 'Newhailes' country house near the city (1686). The third main ecclesiastical style is shown in imposing 19th-century Gothic-revival edifices like Barclay Church (Edinburgh, 1864 – though the style is most famous in the city's Scott Monument) and the wonderful designs of Alexander 'Greek' Thomson (1817–75), notably in St Vincent Street and Caledonia Road, Glasgow.

The last real private castle built from new was Craignethan (Lanarks.) in the 1530s, but the advent of large-calibre gunpowder weapons rendered such fortifications obsolete. In any case, society slowly became more peaceful and landowners preferred tower houses, some of the later ones with windows towards ground level (Elcho Castle, Perths.) before moving eventually to Palladian mansions of varying levels of grandeur. Fashion went full circle with the Victorian 'baronial revival' producing piles like Balmoral and domestic homes too: rambling, fanciful pseudo-castles which, for example, currently house a number of departments of the University of St Andrews on The Scores, these originally built for jute magnates whose factories were in far less salubrious Dundee.

Palladianism is a 16th-century Italian classical-revival style that flowered in 17th-century England before reaching Scotland c. 1680. It is usually called 'Georgian' because it flourished during the reigns of the four British kings of that name (1714–1830). Building on the achievements of Sir William Bruce (c. 1630–1710) and others, its finest exponents were William Adam (1684–1748), who designed gems like Duff House (Banffs.) and the House of Dun (Angus), and his son Robert (1728–92), who designed Edinburgh's Charlotte Square and Register House, home to the National Archives of Scotland. The landed, professional, and mercantile classes wanted Palladian regularity in their townscapes too, exemplified in the New Town of Edinburgh, but also in Perth and to a lesser extent in many other old-established burghs. Vernacular urban architecture of the 15th to 17th centuries featured less imposing, but cosier, small-windowed, and small-roomed houses of rough stone (for example, at Culross, Fife).

For all the prominence of Georgian architecture, Victorian buildings account for the vast bulk of pre-modern erections. Glasgow's Victorian public buildings are Scotland's most glorious, notably the palatial City Chambers in George Square (1888) and Kelvingrove Museum (1901), built to celebrate the city's prosperity and to announce the political and cultural claims of its bourgeoisie. Department stores like Edinburgh's Jenners (opened in the 1830s and rebuilt after a fire in 1895) allowed well-heeled ladies to shop in style.

Even when they dropped, citizens could contemplate their success. Glasgow's Victorian necropolis – an up-market, interdenominational cemetery which, like most Scottish graveyards, was not consecrated ground – was built on a hillside across the road from the cathedral with the graves lined up to afford a view of the city below, rather than lying in the more conventional Christian feet-to-the-east manner. Cremation was introduced in Victorian times and is now the most common means of disposing of the dead.

The substance of the Victorian era was lightened by the recognizable design of Charles Rennie Mackintosh (1868–1928). He got few architectural commissions, but fine examples include Glasgow School of Art (1899) and Hill House, Helensburgh (Dumbartons., 1902). Mackintosh exemplified Art Nouveau's integration of interior and exterior design, of form and function, yet, while visually stunning, his furniture was neither well made nor terribly comfortable. A more commercially successful arts-and-crafts architect was Sir Robert Lorimer (1864–1929), who owned Kellie Castle in Fife and designed the Thistle Chapel adjoining St Giles' Cathedral in Edinburgh, as well as elegant homes across the Lowlands.

There was extensive building of anonymous suburban bungalows in the 1930s when interest rates were low and labour cheap, but distinctively Art Deco buildings are easy to miss, often falling into neglect. Cinemas, ice rinks, roadhouses, and public buildings like Chirnside School (Berwicks.) and St Andrew's House (Edinburgh) exemplify the style. One cannot miss the eyesores erected between the 1950s and 1970s. Touted as 'the gateway to the Highlands', Fort William's main street is an horrific testament to 'planning' gone wrong. The University of Edinburgh gaily demolished the south and east sides of George Square, one of the jewels of the southern or 'first New Town' (1740s and 1750s, whereas the more famous northern 'New Town' of Charlotte and St Andrew Square is 1760s onwards) to build a library and teaching accommodation in the neo-brutalist style.

Scotland's post-war 'new towns' – Cumbernauld, East Kilbride, Glenrothes, and Livingston – were better than inner-city slums and seen as the epitome of enlightened planning at the time, but were also largely devoid of character or public facilities. On the east side of Glasgow, battalions of soulless high-rise flats were created (also with the best of intentions) to re-house inner-city dwellers from areas like the Gorbals, where many flats still lacked indoor toilets. Towns are only now clearing the monstrous carbuncles of this period and, while the architecture seldom reaches the quality of some of Glasgow's recent riverfront developments, it is at least in tune with their historic buildings. Among interesting modern architecture is Dundee Contemporary Arts (1999) and, in Edinburgh, the Museum of Scotland (1999), linked to the adjacent Royal Museum (1888) with its exhilarating main hall. The most controversial modern design is Catalan architect Enric Miralles' Scottish Parliament in Edinburgh, finished embarrassingly behind schedule in 2004 and wildly over-estimate.

Literature, poetry, and film

The first Scottish printing press dates to 1507, and early printing was mainly for the church, but around 1700 secular works began to outnumber religious ones and to diverge from official to more broadly cultural topics. The 18th century saw a flowering of publication on history, travel, philosophy, science, and, from mid-century, of novels, the new fictional but domestically situated genre. Scotland's most famous novelist is Sir Walter Scott. Scott's novels belong to an age of romanticism and sentimentalism, but they are firmly based in Scots law and society. *The Heart of Midlothian* (1818) is an outstandingly realistic historical novel

12. *Sir Walter Scott*, 1822, by Sir Henry Raeburn. Scotland's foremost writer by its finest painter

about illegitimacy and infanticide, society and the law, that still passes muster, and *Guy Mannering* (1815) has much to say about poor relief and insolvency, the latter close to Scott's heart. The less well known John Galt (1779–1839) also dealt sensitively with the realities of social change, religious tradition, legal structures, and political aspiration.

Better known even than Scott is Robert Burns. Famous for his poetry, Burns was also a collector and disseminator of songs. Elegant, accessible, insightful, and profoundly humane, his sometimes earthy verse covers topics as diverse as democracy and drinking, womanizing and work, church and class. He seems to exemplify what Scots are about, and Scott described him as possessing 'a sort of dignified plainness and simplicity'. His influence on British literary figures of the Romantic revival and beyond was immense and he is *the* Scottish cultural icon.

Many authors initially published novels by instalments, and most literature of the 18th and 19th centuries was not weighty and worthy tomes, but bite-sized pamphlets of roughly 16–64 pages. Some had a serious religious, moral, or political point, but many such 'chapbooks' were entertaining, often humorous accounts of life, love, and death. Indeed, humour has been an important part of Scottish culture throughout the ages. Between 1850 and 1920, many joke books were compiled by men of letters, including clergymen and academics, to amuse, but also to celebrate what they saw as the strengths of a passing national character: self-deprecating, decent, and direct. By the late 1920s, Valentines of Dundee were successfully marketing books of Doric jokes in standard English throughout the empire. Scotland's most famous modern comedian is Glasgow-born Billy Connolly (1942–), now happily exiled in the USA. Justly the most famous Scottish film actor, and once tipped as first president of an independent Scotland, is Sean Connery (1930–), who *is* Ian Fleming's 'James Bond'.

Following on from first-generation Enlightenment periodicals like the generalist *Scots Magazine* (1739–1803) were more focused critical, moral, and social quarterlies like the *Edinburgh Review* (1802–1929) and *Blackwood's Magazine* (1817–1980). Long-lived regular newspapers started in the early 18th century: *Edinburgh Evening Courant* (1718–), *Caledonian Mercury* (1720–), *Glasgow Journal* (1741–), and *Aberdeen Journal* (1748–). All eventually folded or morphed into other titles as numbers grew, and the current best-selling broadsheets are the *Scotsman* (Edinburgh, 1860–), *[Glasgow] Herald* (Glasgow, 1805–), and *Press and Journal* (Aberdeen, 1922/1939–), all with different regional emphases, political stances, and editorial styles. Successful modern Scottish tabloids include the *Daily Record*, which trumpets itself as what 'real Scots' read, and the *Daily Express*.

The electronic revolution has added to rather than subtracted from interest in traditional media and demand for hard-copy print remains robust. Scotland's copyright library, the National Library of Scotland in Edinburgh, was established in 1925 on the foundation of the Library of the Faculty of Advocates (1682), and the two remain like cousins once-removed. Access to this library, the National Archives, and most public museums is rightly free, but users are charged for accessing a national resource such as historic records of births, deaths, and marriages to research their ancestry.

Scots have made important contributions to crime writing since Scott, notably the creator of Sherlock Holmes, Sir Arthur Conan Doyle (1859–1930). Modern popular novelists with international reputations include Ian Rankin (1960–), whose Inspector John Rebus inhabits Edinburgh's seamier side, transposing William McIlvanney's Glaswegian Jack Laidlaw (Glasgow was a lot rougher than Edinburgh in the 1960s and 1970s); Iain Banks (1954–), whose dark imagination explores different aspects of modern Scottish society and psyche (darker still are his spectacular science fiction works, under Iain M. Banks); Alasdair Gray (1934–), best known for *Lanark* (1981), is more original (and eccentric) than either. Irvine Welsh's 1993 *Trainspotting*, about the drug culture of multiply deprived north Edinburgh, was made into a successful film in 1996.

These authors reflect a modern interest in gritty realism that can be found even in Scott, Galt, and Hogg in the early 19th century.

Hogg's *The Private Memoirs and Confessions of a Justified Sinner: Written by Himself* (1824) is, for example, blatantly anti-clerical. George Douglas Brown's *The House with Green Shutters* (1901) offered a superb fictional evocation of the vicious smallness of life in an historic village. Brown shattered the homely, sentimental mould of Scottish Victorian 'kailyard' (cabbage patch) literature. Published for a mainly English and American audience, it is exemplified by J. M. Barrie (1860–1937) and epitomized in *Beside the Bonnie Brier Bush* (1894) by 'Ian Maclaren' (1850–1907). Good Scottish literature of the 19th and 20th centuries has a strong sense of place, and Scotland's great artists, storytellers, and poets (notably Orcadian Edwin Muir) all derive inspiration from the landscape. For Will Maclean, it is the sea, but many are, like most Scots, urban creatures. Well-known Scottish poets since Burns include Norman MacCaig (1910–96), George Mackay Brown (1917–96), and Hugh MacDiarmid (1892–1978).

Historical writing that celebrated identity has been around since the mid-15th century when Walter Bower's multi-volume *Scotichronicon* extolled the glories of the kingdom of Scotland. This matured into a strong Whig and Protestant historiographical tradition exemplified by flourishing historical clubs of the late 18th and the 19th centuries. One aspect of Scotland's late 20th-century cultural renaissance has been history publishing, most luminously the Edinburgh firm of John Donald, started in 1972 by John Tuckwell. Other currently successful historical and cultural publishers adding to the rich store of Scottish contemporary literature include Birlinn, Canongate, and the University Presses of Aberdeen and Edinburgh. *History Scotland* (2001–) is a popular monthly magazine on the model of *History Today* (1951–).

Uniquely in Britain, Scotland has a national historian or 'Historiographer Royal', a post dating from 1681. The English originated the idea under Henry VIII, but lost their historiographer in a spat over sleaze early in the 20th century, just when both Edinburgh and Glasgow universities established chairs in Scottish history to signal a new historical awareness; the Irish never had one. Detractors cast up that the present incumbent is an Englishman (Christopher Smout), but he has served Scottish history well before and since 1993.

Proper history publishing is about scholarship, integrity, and attention to both evidence and context. In contrast, most films about Scotland past and present show a cheerful disregard for fact coupled with cloying sentimentalism. David Niven made us cringe in *Bonnie Prince Charlie* (1948), as did the sanitized Jockism of Ealing Studios' *Whisky Galore* (1949), and the mystical twaddle of *Brigadoon* (1954). Scot Bill Forsyth's otherwise delightful contemporary fairy tales, *Gregory's Girl* (1981) and *Local Hero* (1983), were in the same romantic mould. Even *Trainspotting* transformed the desperate, lonely, and sometimes vicious world of hard-drug abuse into a chummy romp.

As superstitious professional actors allegedly say 'the Scottish play' rather than 'Macbeth', professional historians try not to mention 'the Mel Gibson film'. 'Hollywood in a kilt' (but filmed mostly in Ireland, where the tax breaks are better), *Braveheart* (1995) is an enjoyable Highland fling, but laughably inaccurate, hardly a scene without a travesty. To take just the alleged women in his life, there is no hard evidence that William Wallace had a wife, let alone that she endured '*droit de seigneur*' on her wedding night (the idea of the 'first night' was a Victorian hang-up); she is shown being buried in a 'long-cist' grave characteristic of AD 400 not 1300; he cannot have met Isabella, let alone committed adultery with her (she married Edward II in 1308, three years after Wallace was executed).

Peter Watkins' 1964 anti-war *Culloden* is a noble exception to everything before and much since. The first 'docudrama', its raw realism lifts it far above the glossy sentimentality of most 'prince of the heather' offerings. Watkins evoked the carnage of Culloden using embedded reportage (including Gaelic with subtitles) to create a sense of immediacy and humanity in a brutal battle where the Hanoverians lost perhaps 150 men and the Jacobites ten times as many. More is still being found out about Culloden, often by archaeologists, meaning that understandings change, but Watkins was as true to the historical evidence as he could be.

Watkins stood on the shoulders of Scot John Grierson (1898–1972), who may have 'invented' the documentary, but his dreary monologues were a penance for viewers of Scottish television's *This Wonderful World* (1957–67). Engaging yet academically rigorous television history is produced now, notably the 2001 BBC series fronted by Fiona Watson of Stirling University, but there are also get-rich-quick archaeology programmes.

Music

Classical music was played in private houses then, with the commercialization of leisure from the late 17th century, at public venues such as St Cecilia's Hall in Edinburgh's Old Town. Church music too was important. Protestantism is the religion of the book and Bible reading was surely important to faith, but the characteristic Calvinist rituals were catechism (verbal responses to questions about religion) and the singing of psalms. Psalm-singing was a powerful political symbol for Covenanters, and those who wanted a job as a schoolmaster and precentor had to have a good voice, carrying on the pre-Reformation tradition of church song schools teaching chanting, which was important to the Mass and divine office. In its diverse expressions, church music was a vital and varied cultural form.

Yet singing psalms and hymns marked the godly off from the world of harvest ballads and other secular songs, some of them as bawdy in their way as modern rap lyrics. Music for the workplace included narrative 'waulking' songs about domestic issues like marital problems, sung in the 18th and 19th centuries while

groups of women fulled cloth, and the 'bothy ballads' of complaint
and celebration, sung by unmarried farm labourers to tell of
everything about young adulthood, from good times to bad
employers – all with a sense of poignancy that transcends simple
modern romanticizing of the genre. Pastoralism characterized
Victorian and Edwardian music, as it did much visual art.

Other than in church or when pretending to know more than the
first verse of 'Auld Lang Syne' (or karaoke), participative singing
is less usual now than it was before radio and television. Scotland's
national anthem is still officially that of the United Kingdom, 'God
Save the Queen'. More commonly heard now on occasions like
sporting internationals is 'Flower of Scotland', written to celebrate
Bannockburn by successful folk duo The Corries in 1966, which
has eclipsed other contenders like 'Scotland the Brave' (Cliff
Hanley, 1950s). Maudlin expatriates may prefer Dougie MacLean's
'Caledonia', written in the 1970s, but popularized by Frankie
Miller for a lager advertisement (1992).

Traditional Scottish music could be played solo or in a band and
with or without song to accompany dancing or as a one-sided
performance. The harp was the main stringed instrument of
Scotland from the 9th century to the 17th. The principal
instruments of recent times were fiddle, accordion, or concertina,
and chamber pipes as well as bagpipes and possibly a percussion
implement. A wind instrument that uses an inflated bag, bagpipes
are first depicted in the 14th century and are not uniquely
Scottish, but are also found in Ireland, Eastern Europe,
north-west Spain, and parts of Italy. Bagpipes were banned as
seditious after the 1745 Jacobite rising, but reappeared after 1782
(with drums) in British military bands. Pianos were a rarity in
traditional music and guitars a 1960s introduction.

Dynamic, participative, and responsive, so-called 'traditional
music' is far from fixed. Musical inspiration came from native
roots, notably the legendary Shetland fiddler Aly Bain, but also

from Irish folk. Groups like the Battlefield Band and the Boys of the Lough have been enduringly popular leaders of this happy fusion. Folk is now mainstream, though for decades it was classed by some as '*teuchter*' music (a disparaging term, like yokel). There was a distinct pecking order in traditional music depending on the instrument, who played it, by what rules, and where. Robin Hall and Jimmy MacGregor were successful in the 1960s and 1970s, playing to small audiences at the intimate venues that were normal for all musical performances until the advent of stadium rock.

From the 1960s, Scots began to produce their own versions of pop and rock. In the 1960s, there was Lulu, an invaluable TV antidote to the tartan tedium of Andy Stewart (1933–93), himself in the Jockist tradition of Harry Lauder (1870–1950). Glasgow nurtured the likes of Aztec Camera, the Incredible String Band, and Nazareth. There was, regrettably, Edinburgh's Bay City Rollers (the 1970s everywhere was the decade taste forgot), but remember too seminal punk bands like the Rezillos and The Skids. Among the most influential since then, if not the best-selling, are The Cocteau Twins, The Waterboys, and Belle and Sebastian. Texas, fronted by Sharlene Spiteri, and Travis are the most commercially successful of the more serious bands, as were Simple Minds and the duo Eurythmics in their day; Franz Ferdinand looks like going the same way. Some have mass appeal, but limited originality, like Deacon Blue and Wet Wet Wet.

The Scottish part of Scotland's cultural renaissance since the 1980s has been incidental rather than central, but the two best claimants to being distinctively 'Scottish' in a music culture increasingly standardized by commercial pressures are the Proclaimers duo (Lowland, from Auchtermuchty in Fife) for their ethical, home-boy lyrics (you can hear the Scottish accents) and the band Runrig (Highland) for their intense, vibrant songs, many in Gaelic. These participants in global musical culture show how lively and distinctive accommodations have been reached between

Scotland's cultural past and the homogenizing influences of modern media capitalism.

Sport

Soccer may not be 'the beautiful game' for Scots as it is for English, but it is taken very seriously and the feeling that the national side *should* do well has an historic foundation. Between 1296 and 1547, the Scots and the English fought 19 battles, of which England won 11 and Scotland 8. Between the middle of Victoria's reign and the end of Thatcher's, England won 44 football matches played with Scotland, Scotland 40, and 24 were drawn. Though the top clubs (Rangers and Celtic) are European-class, Scotland's national football team has in recent years required more giving than taking, and forays into the World Cup have invariably begun in joy and ended in tears. The coach of the failed Scotland squad in Argentina (1978) was described as less a manager than 'a professional cheer leader'.

The year 1873 saw the founding of the Scottish Football Association (SFA). Established in the same year, the Scottish Football Union (SFU) represented 'football' proper – rugby or 'rugby union'. The SFU became the Scottish Rugby Union in 1924, and Scotland's national rugby stadium opened at Murrayfield in Edinburgh in 1925 (rebuilt 1983). The SFA legalized payments to players in 1893, but rugby stayed militantly amateur until 1995. It is played mainly by the former pupils of elite schools, at university and after, but is also very popular (and more socially inclusive) in the Borders. While popular in the north of England, rugby league never caught on in Scotland. International matches at Murrayfield and across Britain and Europe display only genteel xenophobia compared with their soccer equivalents (or, for that matter, many inter-club conflicts across Britain).

Scots invented golf in the 15th century, but kings frowned on it for interfering with archery practice. It has swanky, invitation-only clubs such as the all-male Royal and Ancient of St Andrews (there is a lady's equivalent and suffragettes had ambushed Cabinet members on-course in the 1900s), but through multiple public courses (including the Old Course at St Andrews) it is cheaper and more accessible, and thus more widely played, than in most places in the world.

Scotland has some outstanding athletes, while lesser-known sports such as curling and shooting spawn world-class competitors and the country produced some decent skiers in the days when there was snow. In 2004 and 2005, a team led by the Duke of Argyll won the world championship of elephant polo in India. One is pleasantly surprised by the existence and occasionally the showing of the national cricket team. Bizarrely, some of Scotland's best-known 'sportsmen' are darts and snooker players.

Sheep were the first quadruped winners of the Highland clearances, but they were superseded by sport animals in the late 19th century as Australian wool displaced Scottish in cloth-making, turning the Highlands into a massive theme park for the rich. By 1884, 'deer forests' covered two million acres or one-tenth of the land. Fox-hunting with hounds was banned in 2002, principally because its social constituency was too small, but angling thrives and the annual slaughter of grouse, pheasants, and deer by well-heeled predators is not only tolerated, but encouraged in the interests of tourism.

Conclusion: The lessons of history

What are the implications of the past for Scotland's future? First, Scots retain a deeply embedded sense of history, albeit a selective one. Like others in the Anglo-Saxon world, they understandably seek identity, empathy, and meaning for their private present by researching family or local history and they want to know about wars and history's celebrities. They are less interested in the public past that creates the context for the social and political present, including for Scotland a separate national church, a distinctive legal code, and a very different experience of government. This detachment may be linked to any number of factors – a preoccupation with individual personal authority, disenchantment with politics, secularization, and electronic communications – but its effects are clear. Yet Scots still feel themselves touched by history and that awareness is a strong part of their identity. Modern Scotland is solidly grounded on historical foundations and the continuity this provides helps in dealing constructively with change.

One manifestation of the public past is a firm civic sense, which helps Scotland's communities to score highly in polls of the most desirable places to live in Britain. Coupled with this is the enduring importance of locality and all the variety and the non-national solidarities it implies. An important reason Scottish devolution has worked so well is that historically Scotland had less centralized government than England and there was an effective civil society: precisely those forms of association below and outside the apparatus of the state, such as churches, communities, and families, mediating between public institutions and private lives, which now so concern the modern West. The notion of civil society empowering citizens has appeal both to the New Right and to left-leaning communitarian ideas of voluntary association, because it insists that people cannot have rights without responsibilities and that individualism has to be tempered by acknowledgement of a common good. Based on their historic experience of government, Scots felt that central authority could and should intervene for benign ends, but that most power should be diffused.

This appreciation of civil society is not rose-tinted. Scotland's history has a dark side of greed, social inequality and injustice, the oppression of women, children, and other races, and bigotry towards different faiths, all repulsive to modern sensibilities. In the present too, there has been sleaze (notably in Labour's 'one-party states' in west-central Scotland), there is a legacy of social conservatism that may encourage ignorance and intolerance, and there are problems of drug and alcohol abuse, anti-social behaviour, and crime, like anywhere in Britain. 'The street', once indicative of intimacy, has become a by-word for danger. Yet a vivid sense of the past, a firm national identity, and a strong civil society rooted in locality mark out both historic and modern Scotland.

History touches modern politics too, for as well as being Scottish, many Scots also feel British. The most important implication is that Scotland's near-term future is unlikely to involve shunning community with the rest of Britain, because it has for hundreds of years been locked into a British paradigm. That does not mean Scots are always comfortable with their past or present relations with England, and they have never been slow to speak out when they perceive injustice. Less laudably, they have long played a 'blame game' against their neighbours. History shows they have a point, but to be a victim is to deny oneself agency. Better to accept how much has been gained from association with England, to recognize what is shared, to take justified pride in what is good about being different, and to change what is not.

The political implications of Union with England are still being played out three centuries on, albeit in a very different world. The component parts of Great Britain (and Ireland, both before and after independence in 1922) developed separately, but they also progressed together in ways that modified their experiences. In some regards, the parts have grown closer over time, but in important ways they remain different. All modern states are artefacts based on conquest and colonization, and laboriously created national solidarity (including Scottish, English, and British identity). Held together for centuries, the integrity of states everywhere is now maintained only precariously, their sovereignty and supposedly inviolable borders steadily eroded. Easy travel, immigration, trans-national crime, and global terrorism, capitalism, and environmental degradation are challenging and complicating our understandings of geography and politics. After 500 years of multi-national accretion, nation states, including Britain, are crumbling back into their component parts. Founded on centuries of uncertainty, experimentation, and compromise, the relations between Scotland and England remain open-ended.

During that time, Scotland has not been a backward version of England waiting to catch up, but something quite distinct. Politically, Scots have known what it is to be both independent and semi-detached in a way that is less true of Wales (whose institutions, if not its language, culture, and habits, were more completely assimilated) and wholly untrue of English regions since the early Middle Ages. Naturally the past should not determine the future, or we should never have shaken off the multiple oppressions of race, class, and gender. But history can liberate as well as limit and attempts to make a destiny that works with rather than against it are likely to be easier, more successful, and longer lasting. If one day Scotland did take the path of independence, it would be as much in tune with its history as would a future within the United Kingdom.

References and further reading

R. D. Anderson, *Education and the Scottish People, 1750–1918* (Oxford, 1995), is best on institutional aspects.

I. Armit, *Celtic Scotland* (London, 1997), is a brief and sensible analysis of this misunderstood period.

G. W. S. Barrow, *Kingship and Unity: Scotland, 1000–1306*, 2nd edn. (London, 2003), is an invaluable brief study of a vital period.

C. G. Brown, *Religion and Society in Scotland since 1707* (Edinburgh, 1997), is the authoritative survey.

L. Colley, *Britons: Forging the Nation, 1707–1837* (London, 1994), offers a powerful argument about the making of modern Britain.

R. Crawford, *Scotland's Books: The Penguin History of Scottish Literature* (London, 2007), is substantial and authoritative.

T. M. Devine, *The Scottish Nation, 1700–2000* (London, 1999), is a good overview, best on economic and political topics c. 1770–1914.

R. A. Dodgshon, *From Chiefs to Landlords: Social and Economic Change in the Western Highlands* (Edinburgh, 1998) is demanding, but deeply rewarding.

M. Fry, *The Scottish Empire* (Tuckwell/Birlinn, 2001), is the most readable survey.

A. Grant, *Independence and Nationhood: Scotland, 1306–1469* (London, 1984), is wide-ranging and thoughtful.

M. Harper, *Adventurers and Exiles: The Great Scottish Exodus* (London, 2003), is a readable general account of emigration, full of human detail.

F. Heal, *Reformation in Britain and Ireland* (Oxford, 2003). The clearest and most dispassionate account: unlike most so-called 'British' history, it does Scotland justice.

J. Hoppit (ed.), *Parliaments, Nations and Identities in Britain and Ireland* (Manchester, 2003). Explores representation before and after 1707.

R. A. Houston, *Scottish Literacy and the Scottish Identity: Literacy and Society in Scotland and England, 1600–1850* (Cambridge, 1985).

R. A. Houston (ed.), *The New Penguin History of Scotland* (Harmondsworth, 2001). A comprehensive, up-to-date, and readable overview, which replaces all earlier single volumes. Now available from the Folio Society.

M. Lynch, *Scotland: A New History* (London, 1991). Probably the best single-author overview, but reflects his expertise on 1400–1700.

A. I. Macinnes, *The British Revolution, 1629–1660* (Basingstoke, 2004), charts how Scots, Irish, and English history became inextricably intertwined.

D. Macmillan, *Scottish Art, 1460–2000* (Edinburgh, 2000). Streets ahead of anything else.

R. D. Oram, *Scottish Prehistory* (Edinburgh, 1997), offers a comprehensive and balanced guide.

L. Paterson, F. Bechhofer, and D. McCrone, *Living in Scotland: Social and Economic Change since 1980* (Edinburgh, 2004), is the best analysis of the dramatic, but still improperly understood, transformation of modern Scotland.

R. Porter, *Enlightenment: How Britain Created the Modern World* (London, 2000), offers a rounded appreciation.

J. Purser, *Scotland's Music: A History of the Traditional and Classical Music of Scotland from Early Times to the Present Day*, 2nd edn. (Edinburgh, 2007), is both readable and comprehensive.

T. C. Smout, *A History of the Scottish People, 1560–1830* (Glasgow, 1972), is outstanding, especially on social history. His *A Century of the Scottish People, 1830–1950* (London, 1986), is also worth reading.

R. S. Tompson, *Islands of Law: A Legal History of the British Isles* (New York, 2000), is a clear and short comparative history of legal diversity, but ...

D. M. Walker, *The Scottish Legal System: An Introduction to the Study of Scots Law* (Edinburgh, 2001), is more definitive on Scotland alone.

M. Watson, *Being English in Scotland* (Edinburgh, 2004), is one of the few serious studies of how the modern English really see the Scots.

C. W. J. Withers, *Gaelic in Scotland, 1698–1981: The Geographical History of a Language* (Edinburgh, 1984).

A. Woolf, *From Pictland to Alba, 789–1070* (Edinburgh, 2007), is an excellent survey of the making of the kingdom.

J. Wormald, *Court, Kirk and Community: Scotland, 1470–1625* (London, 1981), remains the best survey of this important transitional period.

Three ambitious series are in progress. Due for completion c. 2012 is the ten-volume *New Edinburgh History of Scotland*, under the editorship of Roger Mason (Edinburgh University Press). Two other expanding multi-authored collections are particularly useful for social, material, and cultural topics. Planned to be fourteen volumes with seven published so far, *Scottish Life and Society: A Compendium of Scottish Ethnology* (Tuckwell/Birlinn) is an invaluable resource. *The Buildings of Scotland* (Penguin/Yale) is a Scottish Pevsner, not yet national in coverage, but getting there.

Chronology

1018	Malcolm II defeats Angles at Carham
1066	Norman conquest of England
1098	Recognition of Norwegian overlordship of kingdom of Man and the Isles
12th century	Height of Anglo-Norman influence on Scotland
1128	Holyrood Abbey founded
1157	Anglo-Scottish border first fixed at rivers Tweed-Solway
1173–4	William 'the Lion' invades the north of England
1192	Papal bull '*Cum Universi*' recognizes Scottish Church as 'a special daughter'
1237	Treaty of York: Alexander II surrenders claims to northern English counties
1263	Norse defeated at Battle of Largs
1266	Treaty of Perth: Norway cedes Western Isles to Alexander III
1291	Edward I asserts overlordship of Scotland
1295	Franco-Scottish 'auld alliance' formed
1296	Edward I invades Scotland: start of 'Wars of Independence' (to 1328)
1297	William Wallace defeats English at Battle of Stirling Bridge
1305	Execution of William Wallace
1314	Scots defeat English at Battle of Bannockburn
1320	Declaration of Arbroath
1328	Treaty of Edinburgh/Northampton recognizes Scottish independence
1349	Plague arrives in Scotland
1357	Treaty of Berwick: David II released by English
1400	Henry IV invades Scotland
c. 1412	First Scottish university founded (St Andrews)
1469	Annexation of Orkney and Shetland by Scotland (previously Danish)
1472	First Scottish archbishopric (St Andrews)

1493	Lordship of the Isles reverts to James IV
1507	First Scottish printing press
1513	English defeat Scots at Battle of Flodden
1532	College of Justice created
1542	English defeat Scots at Battle of Solway Moss
1544-50	'Rough Wooing' of Scotland
1560	Scottish Reformation
1561	Mary, Queen of Scots, returns to Scotland (deposed 1567)
1590	First major witchcraft trial in Scotland (of North Berwick witches)
1603	Union of the Crowns (James VI of Scotland also becomes James I of England)
1609	Statutes of Iona; Justices of the Peace introduced into Scotland; start of Scottish plantation of Ulster
1622-3	Famine
1633	Charles I crowned in Scotland
1638	'Scottish Revolution' begins the 'Wars of the Three Kingdoms'; National Covenant
1643	Solemn League and Covenant
1645	Last major outbreak of plague in Scotland
1650s	Occupation of Scotland by Oliver Cromwell
1660	Restoration of Charles II
1662	Restoration settlement of religion
1672	Court of Justiciary established
1684	Scots colonies in New Jersey and Carolina
1690	Revolution Settlement of religion
1692	Massacre of Glencoe
1695	Bank of Scotland founded
1695-9	Serious famine and disease mortality
1707	Act of Union: Scottish Parliament merged with English
1708	Scottish Privy Council abolished
1711	Scottish Episcopalians Act
1714	Hanoverian succession to British throne (George I)

1715	First major Jacobite rising (defeated at Battle of Sheriffmuir)
1727	Royal Bank of Scotland founded; last execution of a witch in Scotland
1730s–1790s	Scottish Enlightenment
1733	Original Secession (first major split in the post-Reformation Kirk)
1736	Porteous riots
1746	Last major Jacobite rising, begun in 1745, defeated at Battle of Culloden
1748	Heritable Jurisdictions (Scotland) Act comes into force
1756–63	Seven Years War between Britain and France
1761	Second Secession (Relief Church established)
1776	American Revolution (and War of Independence to 1783); Adam Smith's *The Wealth of Nations* published
1789	French Revolution
1793–1802	Revolutionary War between Britain and France
1800s	First Highland 'clearances'
1803–15	Napoleonic War between Britain and France
1822	George IV's visit to Scotland
1829	Catholic Emancipation in Britain
1832	Parliamentary Reform Act (Scotland); cholera epidemic
1833	Burgh Reform Acts: representative burgh councils established
1842	Edinburgh–Glasgow railway line opened
1843	'Disruption' (Free Church of Scotland established)
1845	Poor Law (Scotland) Amendment Act
1846–8	Peak of Highland famine
1855	Civil registration of births, marriages, and deaths introduced in Scotland
1868	Second Reform Act further extends parliamentary franchise

1872	Education (Scotland) Act makes schooling compulsory
1878	Catholic episcopate restored in Scotland
1884	Further Reform Act creates 'universal' male suffrage
1885	Secretary for Scotland and Scottish Office established
1886	Crofters' Holdings (Scotland) Act
1888	Scottish Labour Party founded
1889	Local Government (Scotland) Act establishes representative county councils
1890	Free schooling introduced; Forth Rail Bridge completed
1899–1902	Boer War
1900	United Free Church formed by union of Free Church and United Presbyterian Church
1914–18	First World War
1918	'Universal' suffrage; Education (Scotland) Act
1922	Labour the largest party in Scotland at general election; first broadcast of BBC from Glasgow
1926	Secretary for Scotland made 'Secretary of State for Scotland'; British General Strike
1928	Male and female franchise equalized
1928/1934	Scottish National Party founded
1929	Reunification of Church of Scotland and United Free Church
1931	National Trust for Scotland founded
1939	Scottish Office moved from London to Edinburgh
1939–45	Second World War
1946	National Insurance established
1947	British coal and electricity nationalized (steel in 1967); first Edinburgh Festival
1948	National Health Service created
1965	Highlands and Islands Development Board established
1967	SNP wins Hamilton by-election; North Sea oil exploration begins
1973–4	International 'oil crisis'

Scotland

Monarchs of Scotland, 843–1714

(Note that early monarchs were kings of only part of Scotland, such as Pictland or Alba.)

MacAlpin or mac Alpín dynasty, 843–1058

Kenneth I	843–58
Donald I	858–62
Constantine I	862–76
Aed	876–8
Giric and Eochaid	878–89
Donald II	889–900
Constantine II	900–43
Malcolm I	943–54
Indulf	954–62
Dubh or Duff	962–6
Culen	966–71
Kenneth II	971–95
Constantine III	995–7
Kenneth III	997–1005
Malcolm II	1005–34
Duncan I	1034–40
Macbeth	1040–57
Lulach	1057–8

Canmore Dynasty, 1058–1290

Malcolm III	1058–93
Donald III	1093–7 (temporarily deposed by Duncan II, 1094)

Edgar	1097–1107
Alexander I	1107–24
David I	1124–53
Malcolm IV	1153–65
William I	1165–1214
Alexander II	1214–49
Alexander III	1249–86
Margaret	1286–90 (interregnum to 1292)

Balliol and Bruce Dynasties, 1292–1371

John	1292–6 (interregnum to 1306)
Robert I	1306–29
David II	1329–71

Stewart Dynasty, 1371–1714

Robert II	1371–90
Robert III	1390–1406
James I	1406–37
James II	1437–60
James III	1460–88
James IV	1488–1513
James V	1513–42
Mary I	1542–67
James VI	1567–1625
Charles I	1625–49
Charles II	1649–85 (exiled during Commonwealth and Cromwellian Protectorate 1651–60)
James VII	1685–8
William II (and Mary to 1694)	1689–1702
Anne	1702–14

Index

Index

Scotland

DRUGS
A Very Short Introduction
Leslie Iverson

The twentieth century saw a remarkable upsurge of research on drugs, with major advances in the treatment of bacterial and viral infections, heart disease, stomach ulcers, cancer, and mental illnesses. These, along with the introduction of the oral contraceptive, have altered all of our lives. There has also been an increase in the recreational use and abuse of drugs in the Western world. This book explains what drugs are, how they work, and how medicines are developed and tested. It also discusses current ideas about why some drugs are addictive, and whether drug laws need reform.

'extremely interesting and capable . . . although called a very short introduction, it contains a wealth of information for the interested layman and is exemplary in its accuracy.'

Malcolm Lader, King's College, London

'a slim but assured and wise volume on drugs. [It] takes up many controversial positions . . . with an air of authority that commands respect. It is difficult to think of a better overview of the field for anyone new to it.'

David Healy, University of Wales College of Medicine

www.oup.co.uk/isbn.0-19-285431-3

INTELLIGENCE
A Very Short Introduction
Ian J. Deary

Ian J. Deary takes readers with no knowledge about the science of human intelligence to a stage where they can make informed judgements about some of the key questions about human mental activities. He discusses different types of intelligence, and what we know about how genes and the environment combine to cause these differences; he addresses their biological basis, and whether intelligence declines or increases as we grow older. He charts the discoveries that psychologists have made about how and why we vary in important aspects of our thinking powers.

'There has been no short, up to date and accurate book on the science of intelligence for many years now. This is that missing book. Deary's informal, story-telling style will engage readers, but it does not in any way compromise the scientific seriousness of the book . . . excellent.'

Linda Gottfredson, University of Delaware

'Ian Deary is a world-class leader in research on intelligence and he has written a world-class introduction to the field . . . This is a marvellous introduction to an exciting area of research.'

Robert Plomin, University of London

www.oup.co.uk/isbn/0-19-289321-1